Death and Marriage Notices of Some Arkansas Baptists

Foreword

The items listed herein were abstracted from photocopies of some Baptist papers issued in the 1850s and following years. Many of these notices were quite long and flowery – so only the genealogical data has been included. The photocopies used were not of great quality and there are, undoubtedly, errors. It is also possible some issues were not copied and presented. The information is presented for whatever benefit it may be to family researchers

(… indicates some text is omitted).

DEATHS

Ashcraft
Mastin Ashcraft died of pneumonia at his residence, Saline County, Ark., February 24th, 1859.
…
Belfast, Ark. March 1st, '59
Arkansas Baptist, March 11, 1859

Poe
James Alferd Poe, son on W. T. Poe, departed this life on the 17th of February, 1859, in the 16th year of his age….

J. Watson

Belfast, Ark., March 1st, 59
Arkansas Baptist, March 11, 1859

Pruit
Died the 5th February, 1859, in Russellville, Pope County, Ark., Mrs. Easter P. Pruit, aged 25 years and 10 months, consort of Dr. J. W. Pruit of the above place.
Arkansas Baptist, March 11, 1859

Dempsey
In this city on Tuesday the 22d February, 1859, in the fifty-first year of his age, Mr. John Dempsey, a native of Little Island, County Cork, Ireland.
Arkansas Baptist, March 11, 1859

Fillingin
At the residence of her mother, Mrs. A. M. Moore, near Ozark, Franklin County, Arkansas, after a lingering illness on the 11th of February, 1859, Mrs. Cornelia E., consort of D. W. Flillingin, aged twenty-six years, eight months, and eleven days.
Arkansas Baptist, March 11, 1859

At the same place, on the 22nd February, 1859, Mary C., infant daughter of the above.
Arkansas Baptist, March 11, 1859

At the residence of M. W. Williams, in Franklin County, on the 2d April, 1857, Cornelia Adaline, infant daughter of the above, aged four months and twenty-seven days.
Arkansas Baptist, March 11, 1859

Davidson
In Mineral Township, Pulaski County, on the 12th of February, 1859, Mrs. Barshabe Davidson, aged 75 years and 9 months.
Memphis papers please copy.
Arkansas Baptist, March 11, 1859

Lee
On the 24th Feb., 1859, in Johnson County, Ark., Mrs. Nancy Lee, wife of Wm. Lee.
Arkansas Baptist, March 11, 1859

Jacques
In this County on the 23d of January, 1959, Mr. William Jaques, aged 60 years. …
Arkansas Baptist, March 11, 1859
Copied From the True Democrat?
Arkansas Baptist July 24, 1859

Searcy
At the residence of G. W. Daugherty, on Friday, July 15th, 1859, Robert C. Searcy, in the 22nd year of his age….
Democratic Sentinel
Arkansas Baptist, July 29, 1859

Pearson
Miss Polly Pearson. Died in Izard County, Arkansas, July 4th, 1859. Miss Polly Pearson, under the charge and roof of Bro. Jacob Wolf. …
Arkansas Baptist, July 29, 1859

Walker
Burwell Walker, died, of old age, at the residence of Elder O. B. Walker, in White co., Ark., on the 16th of Sept., 1859. The deceased was born in Pittsylvania co., Va., June 6th, 1790. Moved to Rutherford co., Tenn., 1818. … Aged, 79 yrs, 8 mos. 10 days. By request of Walker.
Arkansas Baptist, Dec. 16, 1859

Moore
Departed this life, April 25th?, 1860, near Smithville, Lawrence County, Arkansas, infant daughter of William E. and M.A. Moore, aged 6 months and 18 days. …

A.N.E.

Arkansas Baptist, Aug. 8, 1860

Sowell

Mrs. Catharine Sowell: Died. – In this County, on the 29th day of July Mrs. Catharine Sowell, the wife of Mr. Jason Sowell, in the 20th year of her age, leaving an affectionate husband and a small infant, a father, mother, one brother and two sisters …

D.W.S.

Pulaski co., Ark., August, 1860
Arkansas Baptist, Aug. 8, 1860

Moxley

Miss Mary Moxley? Was born in Rockingham co., North Carolina, in October, 1838? She moved to Clarksville, Va., where she remained several years… she moved to Shelbyville, Tenn., In December, 1857?, she came to Arkansas … until the 5?th of April 1861, when death set his seal on her brow. … Her disease was consumption …

Mary & H. McCraw

April 8th, 1861
Arkansas Baptist, April 19, 1861

Judkins

Mrs. Sarah D. Judkins.
At the same place, June 16th, 1860, Mrs. Sarah D. Judkins (grandmother of the above mentioned,) Aged 46 years. Sister Judkins was born in Halifax County, Virginia, August 20th, 1813, where she remained until the year 1820 when she was united in marriage to William H. Judkins, and moved from thence to North Carolina, where she lived until the year 1836; she then with her husband and one child, removed to middle Tennessee, DeKalb County, where she resided till the year 1850, when with her husband and 9 children, she emigrated to Lawrence County Arkansas.…
In the year 1854, her beloved husband was taken from her, while a Senator in the legislature at Little Rock. … Sister Judkins leaves nine children, two sisters, and numerous other relatives and friends …

A. N. E.

The *Tennessee Baptist* please copy
Arkansas Baptist, Aug. 8, 1860

DeArmond

Calvin De Armond … departed this life on the morning of June 8th, 1860. He leaves two infant children, and a wife .. He died aged 34 years. We sympathize with his sister Rose Ann, …
Arkansas Baptist, Aug. 8, 1860

April 8th, 1861
Arkansas Baptist, April 19, 1861

Underwood
Died, on Sunday the 31ˢᵗ ult. at Helena, Ark., Judge A. G. Underwood, of that city….(rheumatism) (had "companion" of over forty years and one daughter)
Helena Note-Book
Arkansas Baptist, Apr. 19, 1861

MISSING YEARS

Evans
Louisiana, daughter of Thomas and Nancy Vann, and wife of James M. Evans, was born December 17ᵗʰ , 1828, in Edgecomb County, North Carolina, and in 1837 her parents moved with her to Haywood County, Tennessee. …she married her now bereaved husband, Jas. M. Evans, who, in November 1896, moved to White County, in this state, and settled near El Paso, … where she remained until the day of her death, May the 28ᵗʰ, 1874. She had a long and protracted illness, which is common in cases of consumption, … Sister Evans was the mother of ten children, two of whom died in infancy, leaving four girls and four boys with the bereaved husband to …

C.

Arkansas Baptist,?, Sept. 26, 1874

Travis
Mrs. Virginia Travis, wife of A. Travis, of Woodruff County, on the 15ᵗʰ inst., of Pneumonia, after an illness of nine days. She was born in Shelby County, Tennessee, on May 5ᵗʰ, 1830-… Mrs. Travis once lived in Searcy, … She leaves an affectionate husband and five children to mourn their loss.
Western Baptist, Jan. 20, 1876

Henley
A Sad Occurrence
Mr. B. F. Henley, an old citizen of this place, and a man highly respected, committed suicide last Monday. Mr. Henley had been partially deranged for some time, and last Monday morning locked himself up in his crib and stabbed himself in the breast with a knife, aiming, as is supposed, to reach his heart, and then cut across his breast. He was not found until late in the evening, was yet alive but speechless. A physician was immediately called in but too late; he died the next evening. …
Western Baptist Jan. 27, 1876

Hays

In this city on the 6th inst., of consumption, Miss Emma Geneva Hays, aged 20 years and 1 month:

Sister Hays was born in Lyon County, Ky., February 6, 1856; in 1869 … In 1871 she moved with her parents to Louisville, .. moved to Little Rock in 1875, …

B.

Western Baptist, April 12, 1876?

Kellem

The wife of Rev. James P. Kellem, of Searcy, died last Sabbath morning at 3 o'clock. She was sixty four years old, …

Western Baptist, April 24, 1876

Brockman

It is with sad heart that we record the death of our much esteemed brother, Henry Brockman, of Garnett, Ark. He died, as we learn, May 27th, very suddenly. He had a father and brother who both died Baptist preachers in Missouri. … bereaved wife and children.

Western Baptist? Aug 17, 1881

Crawford

In Memorium

Crawford, Mrs. P. K., wife of Eld. W. W. Crawford, did a the family residence in South Dardanelle at_ o'clock Friday night, January 27th, Oct. 25th 1815. Her maiden name was Thurmond. She was married to Eld. W. W. Crawford May 14th 81844, Mount Lenon?, Claiborn (now Beinville?) Parish, La She was a widow at the time, having been married to James Hunnicutt, by whom she had two children, and husband and children had died.

By the last marriage (with Eld. Crawford), she had four children, two of whom died young and sleep in Minden?, LA. One, a son, died a martyr to the Confederate cause—serving as a young soldier in Tennessee, and the other, a daughter, lies at the side of the mother in our Dardanelle? cemetery. The deceased daughter left two children …

Arkansas Baptist,?, Feb. 8, 1882

Carolan

Mrs. M. A. Carolan was born Feb. 4, 1842, and died Nov. 9, 1881, aged 39 years, 9 months and 15 days. …She leaves a devoted husband, and four affectionate children to mourn her loss; and four children preceded her to the better land…. She was most happily married to Wm. B. Carolan on the 11th of Nov. 1857, …(leaves husband and children) …

Arkansas Evangel, Feb. 22, 1882

Screeton
Died. At Carlisle, Ark., July 28, little Bertie, youngest son of Geo. T. and Callie Screeton, ages one year and ten months. Disease—cholera infantum.

Mrs. M. A. Muzzy

Arkansas Baptist, Aug. 17, 1882

Wharton
Mary Victoria, daughter of A. J. and M. L. Wharton, aged six years, ten months and fifteen days. Swamp Fever was the destroyer, …
Arkansas Baptist,?, Nov. 16, 1882

From the Texas Baptist: –
Buckner
H. F. Buckner, Deceased…He died at 3 o'clock A.M. December 2, and was buried on Monday, Dec. 4, at 3 P.M. … family; a wife, two daughters and four sons, the oldest being only about nine years old.
Arkansas Baptist, Dec. 14, 1882

Anderson
Captain Monroe Anderson died in Marianna, Ark., of typhoid malarial fever, June 29th , 1882, aged 43 years. He was born in Lebanon, Wilson County Tenn, May 1839, and was educated at Chapel Hill, N. C. A true patriot, he answered his country's call and was a fearless soldier during the civil war.
Moving to this state in the fall of 1864, … married Miss Mooney in the fall of '66, who with two sons now mourn his death, three children having preceded him across the Jordan….[lawyer]

G.A.G.

Arkansas Baptist, Jan. 18, 1883

Craig
Martha O. Craig—Wife of Eld. J. T. Craig, April 2nd, 1883. …Sister Craig moved to our State with her father, in the early settlement of our country,…(pneumonia) three daughters, and as many, or perhaps more than that number of sons, her devoted and mourning husband, and many loving friends,… In July of this year, she would
have been 64 years old.
Arkansas Baptist, Apr. 2, 1883

Martin
Mrs. Sallie Martin – of pneumonia, At Lonoke, April 3, 1883, in the 37th year of her age. … leaving a husband, three sons, an only brother, …
Arkansas Baptist, April 26, 1883

Halbert/Herbert??

At Prattsville, Ark., on the 7th day of Feb., of typhoid pneumonia, Miss Barker Herbert, in the 42nd year of her age. Miss Halbert was born in the State of Mississippi, in the year 1840. She moved to this State with her parents when quite young, … She leaves many brothers and sisters …

Arkansas Baptist, June 21, 1883

Humphries

Samuel O. Humphries, at Searcy, White County, Arkansas, January 6, 1883, aged 11 years, 9 months and 5 days….

W.H. Evans
J. F. Waford

Comm.
Arkansas Baptist, July 12,1883

Lang

Louisa M. Lang, wife of B. F. Lang, on the evening of July 17th, after an illness of two weeks. …Sister Lang leaves a sorrowing husband and four children, an aged mother, brothers and sisters …

R. H. Waddell

Wallaceburg, Ark.
Arkansas Baptist, Aug. 9, 1883

Hughs

Mary Magdalien Hughs, at her residence in Pope County, aged 71 years and 10 months. … She was the mother of twelve children, four of whom she survived leaving eight to mourn her loss in tears. …

Her affectionate son, I.? A. H.

Arkansas Baptist, Aug. 9, 1883

Timms

With deep sympathy for Dr. T. B. Timms and his wife Mrs. Mira Timms, of New Edinburg, Arkansas, we record the death of their infant son, Ben Timms, born April 23, 1882 and died Oct. 12, 1883….

His Pastor.

Arkansas Baptist, Oct. 25, 1883

Searcy

Searcy and was in her eighteenth year, …

L.C.

Arkansas Baptist, Jan. 17, 1884

Moran

Rev. M. Y. Moran

Elder M. Y. Moran, who departed this life on the 23rd day of November, 1883, at his home in Lincoln County, Ark., at the mature age of sixty-five years and seventeen days, …

Arkansas Baptist, Feb. 14, 1884

Lloyd

Mrs. Sarah Lloyd, wife of Thos. Lloyd, died at her home in Logan County, Ark., near Magazine, Dec. 14, 1883. She was born in Wayne County, Ky., Dec. 17, 1817. Her father, Mr. Mann, moved to Jackson County, Ala., in or about the year 1820. where she was brought up to her marriage which took place Aug. 21, 1834. She was married by Joshua Mann, Esq.…

Her husband, Thos. Lloyd, with her and family, moved to Independence County, Ark., in 1849 … She was the mother of twelve children, nine boys and three girls, all living but one. She lies by his side in the cemetery at Magazine … On the 21st of Jan. 1884, the writer of this sketch assisted her husband and son George, with others to place a beautiful tomb stone to her memory.…

Arkansas Baptist, Feb. 28, 1884

McCann

March 2nd, 1884, at 8 o'clock, p.m., Mrs. Sallie McCann, wife of James McCann. … She left a husband and five little children and other friends.

S. N.McCann

Arkansas Baptist, Apr. 2, 1884

Files

At the residence of his brother, Calhoun County, Ark., John M. Files, son of Rev. A. and Sarah Files. He was born in Tuscalusa, Ala., May 8th 1851, his father moved to Arkansas with his family in 1869. He departed this life Feb. 2nd 1883 after an illness of thirty days, aged 26 years, 8 months and 6 days. …

G. B . Talbott

Arkansas Baptist, Apr. 3, 1884

Files

At Fordyce, Dallas County, Ark., Feb. 8th 1884, T.M. Files, son of R. and M. E. Files. He was born Aug. 23, 1859 in the State of Ala., His parents moved to Ark. in 1860. He was 24 years 5 months and 15 days old at his death, …

G. B. Talbott

Arkansas Baptist, Apr. 3, 1884

Robinson

With a sad heart we chronicle the death of Mr. C. C. Robinson, sheriff of Bradley County, who died on the 23rd of April. …[survived by] wife, and aged mother, and other relatives.

Arkansas Baptist, May 5, 1884 and May 15, 1884

Wilson

Mrs. Cassie Wilson, wife of our friend and brother, Capt. R. J. Wilson, after a protracted and most painful illness .was relieved of her sufferings last Saturday afternoon. … Mrs. Wilson was an honored and useful member of the Cumberland Presbyterian church, …[survived by husband and children]

Arkansas Baptist, April 30, 1884

Burke

J. J. Burke, Sub Rosa, Ark., died at his residence in Franklin County, the 2nd day of March, 1884, aged 74 years. … He leaves a wife and 9 children (all grown) ...

DATE & PAPER?

Bayless

Mrs. Ophelia Bayless, second daughter of R. and M. S. Levins. Departed this life February 17th. She was born in October1860, … On December 2nd 1883, she was married to Mr. W. R. Bayless of Nashville. [leaves] bereaved husband and aged parents and all who mourn her loss.

J.D.J.

Arkansas Baptist, April 10, 1884, page 3

Smith

Mary Jane Smith, wife of Brother A. J. Smith late of Georgia, departed this list at her late home, Dallas County Arkansas, February 14th, 1884.
She was born in Campbell County Ga. August 12th, 1810, and married Feb. 25th 1860. … She leaves an affectionate husband and eight children with many relatives and friends …

B.N.H.

Arkansas Baptist, April 10, 1884

Hinkle

Mrs. Mary A. Hinkle died Feb.. 20th 1884; aged 63 years, 2 months and 7 days.
Sister Hinkle was born Dec. 24th, 1821 in Lauderdale Co., Ala. While young her parents moved to Hardin County, Tenn. … She was married to Jesse Hinkle, who survives her, in 1856, after which she and her husband came to Arkansas in 1850. …

Arkansas Baptist, April 10, 1884

Taylor

Mrs. Mary M. Taylor, born Oct. 25th, 1824, in Alabama. … She was married to William Taylor in Murphresboro, Tenn. They afterward moved to Missouri then to Pope Co., Ark. And afterwards to Franklin Co., Ark., where she died of measles the 2nd of April 1885….

R.M. Small

Arkansas Baptist, April 17, 1884

Minor

By order of Hopewell Baptist church, in conference, we, as a committee to prepare a short obituary of Sister Mary E. Minor, wife of Geo. P. Minor, who departed this life, April 11th, 1884. … She was married to Brother Minor April 24th, 1874. …

T. W. Branscomb)
A. Shakelford) Com.
A. C. Hayes

Arkansas Baptist, May 11, 1884

McPike

Edward McPike

Missing   text

In Memoriam.

Lumbley

Eld. John W. Lumbley, the subject of this notice, was born in Yazoo County, Miss., July 17, 1855. … Was married to Miss Mamie Burnett Dec. 26, 1882. Graduated at Clinton, Miss, in June, 1884, and drowned in the Saline river in Cleveland County, Ark., while en route to his appointment at Enoff? Church April 10, 1885. …

Arkansas Baptist, May 21, 1885

May 13, 1885

Denson

N. C. Denson

Arkansas Baptist, May 21, 1885
Arkansas Baptist, July 16, 1885

Downs

Eld. J. _____ Downs- Sept.15,

Hempstead co.; b. Ju? 14th 1821, NC.??

Arkansas Baptist, Oct. 22, 1885

Atkinson
Sister Lealor?, wife of our brother, J.G. Atkinson, died in this city the 3rd of March....

L. Quinn

Arkansas Baptist, April 1, 1886

Coleman
At the residence of their grandfather, Eld. R. J. Coleman, on the 11th and 12th of March, little Coleman Crawford, aged about two years and eleven months, and Norman Crawford, aged about one year and eight months, the only children of Benonie and Allie Crawford.... The disease was measles. Both were interred in one grave in Austin cemetery. ...

R. J. C.

Arkansas Baptist, April 1, 1886

Burgess
Mrs. Phebe E. Burgess was born December 13th, 1847, in Lawrence County, South Carolina. She was moved to Arkansas by her parents, L. and Eunice Boyd. ... Mrs. Eunice Boyd, the mother of sister Burgess, was born in Newburg County, South Carolina, February 24th, 1824.... She moved with her husband to Jefferson County, Arkansas, ..., afterwards moved to Pope County, Arkansas, ... until her death January 20th, 1886....They both left a husband and children and a large circle of friends ...

T. W. Branscome,
W. L. Sproles, Com.
A.Shackleford,

Arkansas Baptist, April 8, 1886

Wesson
William T. Wesson was born in Brunswick County, Va., January 11th, 1810; died of organic lesion of the heart, April 10th, 1886, at his residence near Stephens in Ouachita County, Ark. The subject of this notice was married to Miss Eliza J. Ridout in Tenn., Dec. 28th, 1832. ...
Arkansas Baptist, May 6, 1886

Howard
Died, in Little Rock, Ark., May 27, 1886, at midnight, Mabel A. Howard, daughter of J. O. and M. I?. Howard, born August 8, 1872....
Arkansas Baptist, June 17, 1886

Locke

In Alma, Ark., July 28, 1886, Sister Narcissa A. Locke, wife of Col. M. F. Locke.
Sister Locke was born in Marshall County, Miss. in 1810. …She was married to Brother Locke in 1865, and for more than twenty years they have lived in Crawford County. They made the first settlement in what is now the city of Alma in 1869, and in August 873 they, with eleven others entered into the organization of the Alma Baptist church, …

Arkansas Baptist, Aug. 12, 1886

Vann

Louisiana, daughter of Thomas
and Nancy Vann, and wife of James M. Evans, was born December 17th 1828, in Edgecomb County, North Carolina, and in 1837 her parents moved with her to Haywood County, Tennessee. In 1849,… And on the 23d of December, 1851, she married her now bereaved husband, Jas. M. Evans, who, in November 1896, moved to White County, in this state, and settled near El Paso, … where she remained until the day of her death, May the 28th, 1874. … Sister Evans was the mother of ten children, two of whom died in infancy, leaving four girls and four boys with the bereaved husband to mourn …

C.

Travis

Mrs. Virginia Travis, wife of A. Travis, of Woodruff County, on the 15th inst., of Pneumonia, after an illness of nine days.
She was born in Shelby County, Tennessee, on May 5th, 1830-…Mrs. Travis once lived in Searcy, …
r. She leaves an affectionate husband and five children …

Dearmon

Died-January 3d, at the residence of her father, Mr. Jno. S. McDearmon, Judsonia, White County, Ark., Mary Angeline Hanson, wife of Benj. F Hanson. Mrs. Hanson was born in King County, Tenn., Sept. 1869;… and married in 1877. At the early age of twenty-three she is called away leaving a child too young to realize his loss, and one has gone before. …

Crawford

In Memorium.

Crawford-Mrs. P. K., wife of Eld. W. W. Crawford died at the family residence in South Dardanelle at _o'clock Friday night, January 27th, 1882?aged 67 years nine months and two days.

The deceased, Pernelia Key Crawford, was born at Liberty Hill, Edgefield? District, S.C., Oct. 25th 1815. Her maiden name was Thurmond. She was married to Eld. W. W. Crawford May 14th 1844, Mount Lenon?, Claiborn (now Beinville?) Parish, La. She was a widow at the time, having been married to James Hunnicutt, by whom she had two children, and husband and children had died.

By the last marriage (with Eld. Crawford), she had four children, two of whom died young and sleep in Minden?, La. One, a son, died a martyr to the Confederate cause—serving as a young soldier in Tennessee, and the other, a daughter, lies at the side of the mother in our Dardanelle? cemetery. The deceased daughter left two children …

Arkansas Baptist,?, Feb. 8, 1882

Some may be Arkansas Evangel

Wharton

Mary Victoria, daughter of A. J. and M. L. Wharton, aged six years, ten months and fifteen days. Swamp Fever was the destroyer, …

Arkansas Baptist,?, Nov. 16, 1882

Thomas

Sallie Olive Thomas, youngest daughter of W. J. and Sarah M. Kennedy and wife of James O. Thomas was born in Cherokee County, Ala. On the 27th of Jan. 1859. … She was married to James O. Thomas on the 23rd day of December 1877. … she calmly passed away without a struggle, in the triumphs of a living faith at about 3 o'clock p.m. of Oct. 23rd 1882. …

Her brother,
J. E. Kennedy

Amity, Ark.
Arkansas Baptist, Dec. 7, 1882
Evangel?

Russell

William Russell. On October the 20th 1882 Wm. Russell died. He was born in South Carolina; moved to Georgia; from there to Mississippi; from there to Arkansas and from there to Texas and from Texas back to Arkansas where he died. He was 68 years old. … the lone and bereaved widow and children. He was the father of thirteen children, two died when young, eleven raised, all professors. He leaves six living. The oldest is a Baptist minister and a reader of the *Evangel*…. Done in church conference Saturday before Second Lord's Day in November, 1882.

H. H. Russell, Mod.

B. F. Davis, C. C.

Quitman, Ark.
Arkansas Evangel, Dec. 7, 1882

From the Texas Baptist: –
Buckner

H. F. Buckner, Deceased
He died at 3 o'clock A.M. December 2, and was buried on Monday, Dec. 4, at 3 P.M. .. family; a wife, two daughters and four sons, the oldest being only about nine years old.
Arkansas Baptist,?, Dec. 14, 1882

In Memoriam

Beck

Died in Forrest City,. Nov. 24,1882, Eliza Maude, youngest child of J. W. and Alice L. Beck, aged 5 years and 22 days. …
Arkansas Baptist, Dec. 21, 1882

Brantly

Died. Isabella W. Brantly, wife of Louis Brantly at her home in Bradley County, Ark., on th3 29th day of Nov. 1882. She was born in 1809, … left a loving, aged husband, …. She left also two sons and one daughter …

T. I. Pirtle

Will the *Tennessee Baptist* copy?
Arkansas Baptist, Jan. 18, 1883

Coulter

On Sep. 26, 1882, Mrs. Martha Coulter departed this life, age 75. Mrs. Coulter was born in North Carolina, Aug. 30, 1808, … Shortly after her marriage to Wm. Coulter they came to this State, settling in Hempstead County, …

G. A. Moffett

Arkansas Baptist, Jan. 18, 1883

Meek
Mrs. Myra Meek, wife of Capt.? S. T. W. Meek, died in Hamburg, Ark., January 29th, 1883. …
She leaves a large circle of friends, three sons, a daughter, and husband, …

A.J. Fawcett

Pine Bluff, Ark., Feb. 3
Arkansas Baptist,?, Feb. 8, 1883

Owen
Mrs. Dorah Owen. Daughter of Bro. J. Owen, at Cornersville, March 13, aged 15 years…. after a very painful illness of 3 days with spinal meningitis. …

J. B. S.

Arkansas Baptist, March 22, 1883

Craig
Martha O. Craig—Wife of Eld. J. T. Craig, April 2nd, 1883. …
Sister Craig moved to our State with her father, in the early settlement of our country, …(pneumonia) In July of this year, she would have been 64 years old. …
Arkansas Baptist, Apr. 2, 1883

Martin
Mrs. Sallie Martin – of pneumonia, At Lonoke, April 3, 1883, in the 37th year of her age. …
Arkansas Baptist, April 26, 1883

Halbert/Herbert
At Prattsville, Ark., on the 7th day of Feb., of typhoid pneumonia, Miss Barker Herbert, in the 42nd year of her age. Miss Halbert was born in the State of Mississippi, in the year 1840. She moved to this State with her parents when quite young, … She leaves many brothers and sisters to mourn her loss, ..
Arkansas Baptist, June 21, 1883

Humphries
Samuel O. Humphries, at Searcy, White County, Arkansas, January 6, 1883, aged 11 years, 9 months and 5 days….

W.H. Evans
J. F. Waford
Comm.

Arkansas Baptist, July 12,1883

Lang

Louisa M. Lang, wife of B. F. Lang, on the evening of July 17th, after an illness of two weeks.... Sister Lang leaves a sorrowing husband and four children, an aged mother, brothers and sisters …

R. H. Waddell

Wallaceburg, Ark.
Arkansas Baptist, Aug. 9, 1883

Hughs

Mary Magdalien Hughs, at her residence in Pope County, aged 71 years and 10 months.... She was the mother of twelve children, four of whom she survived leaving eight to mourn…

Her affectionate son, I.? A. H.

Arkansas Baptist, Aug. 9, 1883

Toone

Lizzie Toone, on the 4th instance, at Plum Bayou???, Jefferson County, Ark, wife of George W. Toone, formerly of Tulip, Dallas County, Ark. The fatal malady was an ulcer in the stomach. … Her husband and children have our sincere condolence….

R. M. Thrasher

Arkansas Baptist, Aug. 30, 1833

Veasy

A.L.? Veasy, at Warren, Ark., of typhoid fever, August 13th. …Brother Veeasy was born February15th, 1861. … He leaves an aged father and mother and one sister, and a host of friends ..

N. C. Denson

Warren, Ark
Arkansas Baptist, Aug. 30, 1883

Seward

Felix L.? Seward
The above named evangelist, pastor, agent and efficient missionary …
passed away from earth on the 30th day of June last, having lingered for many long years with nervous prostration. He came to Alma, Arkansas…
He left three children and a little granddaughter, besides his circle of friends….

M.F.L.??

[Tenn. Baptist please copy.]
Arkansas Baptist, Sept. 20, 1883

In Memoriam
By Mrs. Lucinda Cooper

Currey

Departed this life August 25th, 1883, Henry R. Currey, son of James W. and Fannie M. Currey, at their residence, near Annover, Dorsey County, Arkansas aged 8 months and 8 days…

Arkansas Baptist?? Nov. 15, 1883

In Memoriam

Searcy

On the morning of Jan. 4, 1884, ten minutes past four o'clock, at her home at Annover, Mollie Searcy3 sweetly fell asleep…She was the eldest daughter of Elder J. B. and Mrs. Fannie Searcy and was in her eighteenth year, …

L.C.

Arkansas Baptist,? Jan. 17, 1884

Moran

Rev. M. Y. Moran

…… Elder M. Y. Moran. who departed this life on the 23rd day of November, 1883, at his home in Lincoln County, Ark., at the mature age of sixty-five years and seventeen days, …

Arkansas Baptist, Feb. 14, 1884

Mcann

Sallie McCann, wife of James McCann. … She left a husband and five little children and other friends to mourn her loss.

S. N. McCann

Arkansas Baptist, Apr. 2, 1884

Files

At the residence of his brother, Calhoun County, Ark., John M. Files, son of Rev. A. and Sarah Files. He was born in Tuscalusa, Ala., May 8th 1851, his father moved to Arkansas with his family in 1869. He departed this life Feb. 2nd 1883 after an illness of thirty days, aged 26 years, 8 months and 6 days. …

G.B . Talbott

Arkansas Baptist, Apr. 3, 1884

Files

At Fordyce, Dallas County, Ark, Feb. 8ᵗʰ 1884, T.M. Files, son of R. and M. E. Files. He was born Aug. 23, 1859 in the State of Ala., His parents moved to Ark. in 1860. He was 24 years 5 months and 15 days old at his death, …

G. B. Talbott

Arkansas Baptist, Apr. 3, 1884

Robinson

With a sad heart we chronicle the death of Mr. C. C. Robinson, sheriff of Bradley County, who died on the 23ʳᵈ of April. … our earnest sympathies to his bereaved wife, and aged mother, and other relatives.

Arkansas Baptist, May 5, 1884 and May 15, 1884

Wyeth

Died suddenly, at this residence in Judsonia, Thursday, April 27, Joseph B. Wyeth. Born in Jefferson County, N. Y., June 1819, he was therefore in his 65ᵗʰ ;year. He removed to Ohio when a boy … In 1840 he was united in marriage to Miss Charlotte Horton, who survives him … In 1850, Mr. Wyeth removed to Charleston, Ill. … to Arkansas in 1871; …

Arkansas Baptist, May 15, 1884?

Miller

Brother John Miller, aged 76 years and 8 months, died of heart disease April 29, 1884….

R. M. Small

Arkansas Baptist, May 15, 1884

Thompson

Died. Eld. William Thompson, at the residence of his son, B. F. Thompson, in Lonoke County, Ark., March 12ᵗʰ , 1884, aged precisely on that day 79 years.

Brother Thompson was born March 12ᵗʰ, 1805, in Christian Co., Ky., and emigrated with his father to Mississippi, … He moved from there to Fayette Co., Tenn., in 1831, was united in marriage to Miss M. L. Hays, who still survives him. … He moved to Arkansas in 1855, …

Arkansas Baptist, Apr. 24, 1884

In Memoriam.

Lumbley

Eld. John W. Lumbley, the subject of this notice, was born in Yazoo County, Miss., Jul7y 17, 1855. …Was married to Miss Mamie Burnett Dec. 26, 1882. Graduated at Clinton, Miss., in June, 1884, and drowned in the Saline river in Cleveland County, Ark., while en route to his appointment at Enoff? Church April 10, 1885. …

Arkansas Baptist, May 21, 1885

Gillis

Brother J. G. Gillis

The subject of this notice was born in North Carolina, May 21, 1819, and died in Bradley County, Ark., April 12, 1885.

He had been afflicted for several years with lung disease, … About 1844 or 1845 he moved to Arkansas and settled in what is now known as Dark Corner, Bradley County, where he engaged in farming. …

A Brother and Friend

May 13, 1885

N. C. Denson

Arkansas Baptist, May 21, 1885

Hays

Our beloved brother, A. C. Hays, departed this life at his residence near Atkins, Pope County, on the 17th day of April, 1885. Aged 47 years, 6 months and 11 days. …

Arkansas Baptist, May 23, 1885

Bright

Died in this city, Saturday 13th inst. At the residence of its parents on State St., the infant son of Mr. And Mrs. W. A. Bright. …

Arkansas Baptist, July 2, 1885

Blackwell

Mrs. Mary J. Blackwell departed this life at her home in Columbia County, March 16, 1885. She was born September 1848, the eldest daughter of Mr. James and Nancy Mexion. .

Arkansas Baptist, July 2, 1885

Minyard

Minyard was born Aug. 11, 1838 in Alabama. She was moved to Miss. At the age of five, and to Clark County, Ark., in 1854. She was the daughter of Jas. and Ann McCraw…. She was married to E. L. Minyard, Oct. 25, 1859. …

G. M. Shaw
J. W. Brock
W. P. Barton
J. H. Wisdon,
Committee

Arkansas Baptist, July 16, 1885

Ingram

On the 25th day of June 1885, God in his inscrutable providence, saw fit to claim, and recall from its tenement of clay, the spirit of Willie Ingram….

A.W. Files,
H. C. Hinton,
Mrs. H. A. Laurie,
Comm.

Arkansas Baptist, July 16, 1885

Stovall

Mrs. Caroline V. Stovall consort of R. A. Stovall died in the town of at her home on the 16th of May 1885. She had been a subject of severe affliction for many years, yet she bore it with great patience. She was born in Grenada, Mississippi on the 17th of April 1839, … .. Was married on the 13th of March, 1959. They soon emigrated to afterward to Lonoke County and Prairie County ????? and settled near where she died. … She left a husband and three children and a large circle of friends …

R. J. C.

Cabot, Ark. June 1st, 1885.

Fox

Mrs. Sallie A. the wife of deacon H. C. Fox, was born in Arkansas May 14th, 1860, and died in Hot Springs May 15th , 1885, aged 25 years, 1 day. …

Arkansas Baptist, July 13, 1885

Bayner

In Little Rock, July 256, 18854, Miss Lida H. Bayner, age 12?,. Only a few months have passed since she was baptized into the fellowship of the First Baptist _____

Arkansas Baptist, Aug. 6, 1885

Threlkell

Mrs. Ida Pearl Threlkell, consort of Mr. DeWitt Threlkell, and only daughter of Mr. And Mrs. A. K. Bollinger, died of congestion at her residence in Russellville Friday evening at 3 o'clock, July 24, 1885....

Mrs. Threlkell leaves a fond father and mother, a devoted husband, two brothers, a little girl, and a large circled of friends here and in Mississippi, ...

Arkansas Baptist, Aug. 6, 1885

Edwards

In Little Rock, September 6, 1885, Mr. R. A. Edwards, in the seventy-third year of his age. ...s of God. He removed from his native State, Tennessee, to Arkansas twenty-six years ago, ... One of his chief afflictions was extreme deafness, ... appropriate services were conducted by Dr. Cornelius. Thence we conveyed the remains of this old pioneer Baptist to their last resting place in Mount Holly cemetery,....

Arkansas Baptist, Sept. 17, 1885

Chandler

Mrs. Alice Chandler, daughter of sister Mary Barnes, was born March 1st 1858 and died near Clinton, Arkansas, August 13th 1885....

Arkansas Baptist, Sept. 24, 1885

Sanders

Died of Dysentary, In Hazen, Arkansas, on the 10th day of September, 1885. Mrs. Eliza C. Sanders wife of Col. R. T. Sanders. Mrs. Sanders , daughter of Gen. David Boone, was born in Johnson County, North Carolina, Oct. 14th, 1814. Married to Reuben Troy Sanders, April 3rd 832. ... To her husband, three living children, many grandchildren, we extend our heart-felt sympathy, .

Lonoke, Ark. Sep. 15th 1885.

Arkansas Baptist, Sept. 24, 1885

Turbervill

Mrs. W. M. Turbervill was born in Columbia County, Ark. in 1862. She was the daughter of Reuben and Rebecca Bearden ... she moved to Washington County ... She was married to A. Turbervill May 1883....

D. N. Mullins

Arkansas Baptist, Oct. 1, 1885

Latourette
In Prescott, Arkansas, September 22nd, 1885, Mr. D. L. Latourette, in the sixty-third year of his age…. He had married a cousin of mine, a daughter of my beloved uncle, the late Rev. John Booth. Mr. Latourette was a man of superior mind and strong will. He excelled as an inventor and as a financier, …
Arkansas Baptist, Oct. 15, 1885

Downs
Eld. J. _____ Downs- Sept.15,
Hempstead co.; b. Ju? 14th 1821, NC.
Crease in copy – difficult to read.
Arkansas Baptist, Oct. 22, 1885

Another Veteran Fallen
Carter
Bro. W. J. Carter died Oct. 9th, 1885, aged 73 years and 7 months.
He was born in the State of South Carolina, in 1812. He moved to Alabama and was wed? to Rebecca Meador in the holy bonds of matrimony. In 1835, … baptized into the fellowship of the Mount Pleasant Church by Elder Kedar Hawthorn, the father of Gen. Hawthorn. …[moved to Nevada County, Arkansas, … He leaves six children and a host of friends …

T. D. Tipton

Mississippi and Texas papers please copy.
Arkansas Baptist, Nov. 5, 1885

Burns
The New Friendship church has sustained a great loss as we deem it in the death of Bro. James A. Barns who died of Swamp Fever at his residence in Saline County. …
May the bereaved wife and orphan children be blessed and comforted by him who is able to comfort us in all our afflictions.

A.T.

Arkansas Baptist, Dec. 10, 1885

Moran
Mrs. M. A. Moran, wife of the deceased Elder M.Y. Moran was born Feb. 23, 1829, died at her home near Star City, Ark., Sept. 27, 1885. ….Mrs. Moran had attended the Friendship Association at Toledo, left there for home on Tuesday, and the next Sabbath, she passed from earth to the spirit-land and joined her sainted husband who had preceded her scarcely two years before….
Arkansas Baptist, Dec. 10, 1885

Davis
John Sidney Davis, the infant son of Eld. I. R. B. Davis and wife, was born Aug. 23, 1884....

Mama.

Hope, Ark.
Arkansas Baptist, March 4, 886

Cullins
In Independence County, Arkansas, December 30, 88, Mrs. Cullins, at the age of 29 years, 9 months and 21 days. She was the daughter of Mr. and Mrs. Gay. ... She left a father and brother and sisters and a host of friends ...

M. L. Bearden

Arkansas Baptist, March 11, 1886

Bozeman
Died at her residence six miles west of Arkadelphia February 5th, 1886, Mrs. Lucy Ann Bozeman, wife of the late Michael Bozeman, aged 72 years 5 months and 8 days. She was born in Green County, Georgia. At the age of 16 years her father John Browning moved to Lowndes County, Alabama. She united in marriage with Michael Bozeman September 27th 1827. ... to Clark County, Arkansas, then a territory, in 1835. ...
Arkansas Baptist, March 11, 1886

Atkinson
Sister Leal?or, wife of our brother, J.G. Atkinson, died in this city the 3rd of March. ...

L. Quinn

Arkansas Baptist, April 1, 1886

Coleman
At the residence of their grandfather, Eld. R. J. Coleman, on the 11th and 12th of March, little Coleman Crawford, aged about two years and eleven months, and Norman Crawford, aged about one year and eight months, the only children of Bennie?? and Allie Crawford....
The disease was measles. Both were interred in one grave in Austin cemetery....

R. J. C.

Arkansas Baptist, April 1, 1886

Craig
Our dearly beloved brother J. T. Craig, departed this life at his residence near Kingsland, Cleveland County, Arkansas, on the 18th day of Dec. 1885. Bro. Craig lived his three score and ten, the time allotted to man....
Arkansas Baptist, April 4, 1886

Renfro
Elder J. C. Renfro, the subject of this sketch, was a native of Kentucky. ... He died at the residence of J. C. Boatright, his son-in-law, January, 1886. ...

D. P. Tupper

Arkansas Baptist, Apr. 4, 1886

Watts
Sister E.E. Watts, of Delta, Nevada County, Ark., died at her home, at Delta, on the 18th day of April, 1885, ... resulting from a severe burn.
Sister Watts was born July the 9th, 1820, and was married in 1843, ...

J. B. Perminter

Magnolia, Ark. April 27, '86
Arkansas Baptist, May 6, 1886??

Wesson
William T. Wesson was born in Brunswick County, Va., January 11th, 1810; died of organic lesion of the heart, April 10th, 1886, at his residence near Stephens in Ouachita County, Ark
Ridout
The subject of this notice was married to Miss Eliza J. Ridout in Tenn., Dec. 28th, 1832. ...
Arkansas Baptist, May 6, 1886

Loyburn
Died – of pneumonia at Lonoke, Ark, April 9, 1886, William Walter Loyburn???, aged 14 years, 4mos., 23 days....

D.A.E.

Arkansas Baptist, May 20, 1886

Kimrough

Deacon Thomas Kimbrough was born in Jefferson County, Tenn., May 2, 1805. Was married to Miss Elizabeth Austell Feb. 14, 1832. … his death which occurred May 12th, 1886. Brother K. was 81 years and 10 days old. Near two years ago while attending a protracted meeting in his church, he had a paralytic stroke; he had a second stroke two months before his death. … His father was Elder Duke Kimbrough, one of the leading ministers of Tennessee in an early day. He was a brother of Elder Bradley Kimbrough, … The Kimbroughs of Texas are of the same family. …

To his seven surviving children, and his many grandchildren,…

J.C.R., His Pastor.

Elm Springs, Ark., May 20, 1886.
Arkansas Baptist, June 6, 1886

Howard

Died, in Little Rock, Ark., May 27, 1886, at midnight, Mabel A. Howard, daughter of J. O. and M. ?. Howard, born August 8, 1872. …
Arkansas Baptist, June 17, 1886

Locke

In Alma, Ark., July 28, 1886, Sister Narcissa A. Locke, wife of Col. M.F. Locke.
Sister Locke was born in Marshall County, Miss. in 1810. …
She was married to Brother Locke in 1865, and for more than twenty years they have lived in Crawford County. They made the first settlement in what is now the city of Alma in 1869, …
Arkansas Baptist, Aug. 12, 1886

Hughes

Deacon L. B. Hughes, near Johnson, Arkansas, March 25, 1890.

Resolution …

Resolved, That the church has lost one of her pillars, the community a valued citizen, the family an affectionate husband and loving father….

G. T. Hanks,
John Busby,
S. Thurmond,
Com.

Arkansas Baptist, June 12, 1890

Dyson

At his home near Dobyville, Ark., June 9, 1890, Prof. John N. Dyson.
He leaves four children without the care or council of a father or mother. Prof. Dyson graduated at Mercer University Macon, Georgia, when only twenty years old....

R. E. Lawlis

Arkansas Baptist, July 17, 1890

Powell

, Mrs. Lula J., wife of John Powell. Born May 19, 1871; died April 21, 1890, at Berea, Arkansas. Sister Powell was a daughter of J. O. and E. A. Riley of Ashley County, Arkansas. ...

S.E.L., a sister

Arkansas Baptist, July 17, 1890

Honea

In Lonoke County, Ark., John L. Honea, May 21, 1890.Bro. Honea was born in South Carolina January 1822, moved to Georgia when seventeen years ... He left an aged widow who is sorely bereft, also nine children, ...

R. J. C.

Arkansas Baptist, July 17, 1890

Galloway

Permelia Galloway, born February 4th 1807; died April 16th, 1890. ...

E. F. Appling

Brooks, Ark.

Arkansas Baptist, July 24, 1890

Byers

Mrs. Ann Byers, at the residence of her son-in-law, Maj. W. White, in Cuero, DeWitt County. Texas. May 5th 1890, aged 64 years. The subject of this notice was born in Knoxville, Tenn. Was married Nov. 15th, 1846, by Rev. J. R. Graves, to W. H. Byers in Nashville, Tenn. About thirty years ago they moved to Fort Smith, and after the war to Crawford County, Arkansas. T... She leaves two sons, three daughters and many friends ...

M. A. B.

Arkansas Baptist, July 24, 1890

Freeman

Freeman- F., died on March 12, 1895. Aged 69 years, 9 months and 9 days. Bro. Freeman was born in Ray County, Tenn., June 8, 1825. … Moved to Arkansas in 1857. … He was married to Elizabeth Sidley, who preceded him about four years. …

W.N. Womack

Morrison's Bluff, Ark.
Arkansas Baptist?, March 4, 1895

Adcock

– J. D., died on March 4, 1895. …

C. M. Powell

Arkansas Baptist,?, March 4, 1895

Barnett

, Ellen E., died at her home in Van Buren County, Ark., March 25, 1895, aged 12 years, 2 months and 25 days. Ellen was born in Etowah County, Alabama, Dec. 29, 1882. She was moved several times, and was finally brought to Van Buren County, Ark., in December, 1890. …" She leaves a father and mother, four brothers, one sister, and a hose of friends behind her. … Funeral services were held by Eld. W. F. Sims.

S.B. Barnett
Her Brother

Arkansas Baptist,?, March 4, 1895

Johnson

Death has again taken from our membership our beloved brother, Eld. W. C. Johnson, who departed this life on Thursday, January 17, 1895?. … He was 72 years old. …

S. H. Weatherly,
John Hammett,
W. T. Allison, committee

Holliday, Ark. (Haliday?)
Arkansas Baptist,?, March 4, 1895

Lett

Lett, Mrs. T. B. died at her home in Little Rock on February 6, 895. …

Frank White

Arkansas Baptist,?, March 13, 1895

Harris

Harris – Augustine, died in Cleburne, Texas, March 12, 1895. Aged 71 years and 8 months. … He was born in North Carolina in 1823; … Two years ago he came to Texas to live with his son, Dr. T. T. Harris, at whose home he died. His son, Eld. Wm. H. Harris, and a younger son in attendance upon a medical school in St. Louis, …

J.W. Newbrough
Cleburne, Tex.

Arkansas Baptist, April 10, 1895

Alford

Alford - Lucy, died at her home in Sparkman, Ark., March 27, 1895. … May the husband and three grown children…

H.J.P. Horne

Arkansas Baptist, April 10, 1895

Quinn

Quinn – Mrs. Nettie, wife of T. W. Quinn, died at her home near Prattsville, Ark., January 30, 1895. Aged 40 years. … husband and two children …

A Friend

Arkansas Baptist, April 10, 1895

Lindsey

Lindsey – R. E. Lee, son of Eld. R.? H. Lindsey, died of consumption March 29, 1895. …
????
Where??

Arkansas Baptist, April 10, 1895

Thomas

In Memoriam…
death has taken from our midst our much loved pastor, Eld. Thomas Hudson; … Bro. Hudson was born at Belfast, Ireland, on March 17, 1827, … studied in the University of Glasgow, Scotland. He came to America in 1865, and has spent the years since in Missouri and Arkansas. … bereaved daughters …

???

Arkansas Baptist, April 16, 1895

Anthony

Foster – Eld. Anthony, died at
Pitman, Ark., April 9, 1895. Aged 65 years, 2 months and 2 days.   Bro. Foster was born January 16, 1830; … d.

T. J. Gambell

Pitman, Ark.
Arkansas Baptist, May 8, 1895

Gage

Gage – Miss Ethel M.? , dau. of Bro. And Sister W. L. Gage, was born December 15, 1870; died March 5, 1895….

C. B. Hunton

Ouachita Ripples please copy.
Arkansas Baptist, March 20, 1895?

Adams

Adams – W. W., died at his home in Warren, Ark., February 28, 1895. Aged 50 years. … He leaves a wife and three children and a niece who made her home with him….

H. A. Munn

Arkansas Baptist, March, 27, 1895

Mack

Mack, Mrs. M. E., of Warren, Ark., died in Paragould March 3,1895. …

Warren Baptist Ladies' Aid Society

Arkansas Baptist, March 27, 1895

Allison

Allison, W.J., son of Cornelius Allison, died December 26, 1895, at the age of 26 years. … He was married to Sister Lucy Eskridge, ….

S. W. Abernathy,

Tuckerman, Ark.
Arkansas Baptist, Jan. 12, 1896

Deer

Deer, Mrs. Sarah J., nee George, died a quiet and peaceful death November 6, 1895, at her home near Lono, Hot Spring County, Ark. She was born September 28, 1845, in Mississippi and moved with her parents to Louisiana and thence to Arkansas; was married to Jas. L. Deer the 3rd of February 1867, …
Arkansas Baptist, Jan. 15, 1896

Hutchins

Hutchins, Mary Lucy. Born in Merriwether County, Ga., March 23, 1877,. Died at her father's home near Columbus, Ark., December 12, 1895, aged 18 years, 9 months and 21 days. ...
Arkansas Baptist, Jan. 15, 1896

Meredith

Meredith, H. H. The sad news of the death of Bro. Meridith, of this County, has just been received. Bro. Meredith has been a citizen of this County for more than forty years, ...
He leaves a devoted Christian wife and three daughters ...

J.G. Copeland

Wolf Creek, Ark.
Arkansas Baptist, Jan. 15, 1896

Sanders

Sanders, Mrs. Louiza Eleanor. Nee Thornbrough, was born in Tennessee October 20, 1832, died at her home in Van Buren County, Ark., January 2, 1896, aged 63 years, 2 months and 12 days.... In 858 she moved to Arkansas, ...

S. R. Barnett

Clinton, Ark
Date not legible

Moseley

Moseley, J. J. Died October 245, 1895, aged 65 years. Bro. Moseley was born in South Carolina January 21, 1830; came to Arkansas in 1851, ... He was a devoted husband, loving father ...

W. H. Cash

Arkansas Baptist, Jan. 15, 1896

James

James, J. C., died November 19, 195, aged 49 years, 7 months and 23 days. ...
Arkansas Baptist, Jan. 15, 1896

Rankin

Rankin, John B., born in Mississippi in 1847; married Miss Elizabeth Moreland in 1877, and moved to Arkansas in 1879. ... He leaves a father, wife, three daughters and four sons to mourn...

J. Eugene Woodruff

Lavaca, Ark.
Arkansas Baptist, Jan. 29, 1896

Moseley

Moseley, Sidney Clark son of Preston C. and Callie Moseley. Born January 20, 1893; died at Altus, Ark., January 6, 1896. …

D. D. Warlich,
Pastor M. E. Church, South

Arkansas Baptist, Jan. 29, 1896

Sypes

Death has again visited our little village and taken from our midst Sister Cora Sypes. … She was an affectionate daughter, sister and friend and the beautiful songs she loved to sing …

W. A. Turnage

Arkansas Baptist, Jan. 22, 1896

Jones

Jones, Ed. S.- January 7, 1896, at his home in Searcy. He was born in Rome, Ga., in 1851; … Besides his wife he leaves a daughter and ___ sons …

E. C. Faulkner

Arkansas Baptist, Jan. 22, 1896
Searcy, Ark. Jan. 16, 1896

Haugh

Our beloved sister, Samantha?Sarah? Haugh, ___ …and on the 11th day of August, 1896, she bid adieu to earth and earthly things, leaving a husband and one daughter …

W. M. Tucker
H. Hales,
Committee

Arkansas Baptist, Jan. 22, 1896

Memoir of Eld. I. R. Vick

Vick

Born June 16, 1830; died November 27,1895, at his home in Lincoln County, Ark. He retired at 9 o'clock apparently well, and went quietly into a sleep from which he never woke. … He was born in Nash County, North Carolina, migrated to Cass County, Ga.,… He moved to Drew County, Ark., in 1860 …

E.Y. A. Rogers

Montongo, Ark.
Arkansas Baptist, Jan. 22, 1896

Gowin

It is with sadness that I write the obituary of Sister A. L. Gowin, wife of Ed. C. Gowin who was taken sick January 18 and died the 19th. She was the daughter of Rev. I. H. Hubbard. Was born in Calhoun County, Ala., in 1852, moved to Arkansas with her parents when but a girl, was married to George Biddle in January, 1871, who died and left her a widow. She was married to Bro. C. A. Gowin on September 17, 1874. Sister Gowin was the mother of eleven children, ten of whom are living. ...

D. A. Squires

Arkansas Baptist, Feb. 19, 1896

King

King – Mrs. Sallie, died at her home in Pine Bluff, Ark., January 7, 1896; aged 46 years. ... To her three children, two sisters and other relatives ...

Mrs. Langston,
Mrs. Will Beard,
Mrs. W. H. Parker
Committee Ladies' Aid Society, Baptist Church, Pine Bluff, Ark.

Arkansas Baptist, March 4, 1896

Hurley

Hurley, William Penn, died at his home near Hickory Grove Baptist church, December 12, 1895, after an illness of only four days. Bro. Hurley was born March 5, 1846 in Dyer County, Tenn.; moved to Arkansas in 1859; was married to Miss Malviny Roberts in 1869. ... The wife is bereft of a loving husband and companion, the children ...

Thomas H. Leeman

Date of paper and location missing

Moffett

A testimonial in memory of little Jeannie Moffett, who was born February 25, 1891 and died February 13, 1896....

Arkansas Baptist, March 4, 1896

Adams

Adams – Mary H., wife of A. E. Adams, was born in 1861.

T. A. Middlebrooks

Arkansas Baptist, March 18, 1896

Goza

Goza – Deacon Mark, died at the home of Mead Williams, his son-in-law, near Donaldson, Ark., March 1, 1896. Aged 92 years, 2 months and 3 days. A native of Georgia, but moved with his parents to Chester, S.C., in 1807. In 1833 he moved to Gibson County, Tenn.; … He moved to Hot Spring County, Ark., in 184?, … He leaves seven children—two sons in Texas (one a Baptist minister); three sons and two daughters in Hot Spring County. …

B. S. Taylor

Donaldson, Ark.
Arkansas Baptist, March 25, 1896

Vaughn

Vaughn – Eliza Green, was born in Georgia November 27, 1839, and died at Stamps, Ark., January 21, 1896. Was married to A. Vaughn September 17, 1870; …
She leaves a husband, daughter and a large circle of friends …

A.T. Dodd,
B. Taylor Calhoun,
committee

Arkansas Baptist, March 25. 1896

Mitchell

Mitchell – Enoch, was born in Poinsett County, Ark. October 11, 1827, and died at his home in Harrisburg, in the same County, February 5, 1896. He was married to Miss Catherine Greenwood, March 1, 1848. Bro. Mitchell was three times elected treasurer of Poinsett County, and did for many years an active and upright mercantile business….

A Friend.

Arkansas Baptist, April 1, 1896

White

White – Laura E., daughter of G. C. and N. A. White, was born April 24, 889 and died March 20, 1896. … Father, mother, brogthers, sisters and friends …. The funeral services were conducted by the writer, J. T. Gossett,
March 21.
Arkansas Baptist, April 1, 1896

Mann

Mann – Sister Mary E., was born in Georgia September 12, 1831; … and she was married to Jas. Mann July 20, 1851. To them were born six children, three of whom passed over the river while young and three are living, to-wit: Mrs. Si. Boss, Mrs. George Suttle and J. A. Mann, now of Ft. Smith. Sister Mann died February 3, 1896, …

J. N. Pennington.

Arkansas Baptist, April 8, 1896

Quinn

Quinn, T. W., Jr. – Died at Prattsville, Ark., On the 18th of February ult. Of malignant tumor of the bowels, in the 26th year of his age. Deceased was born and reared here,…
Two years ago he was united in marriage to Miss Mattie Messenger, of this place by whom he left one little boy to survive him.

.A Friend

Arkansas Baptist, April 8, 1896

Jones

Jones – Mrs. Maggie, died at her home in Searcy, Ark., March 25, 1896. Her husband, Bro. Ed S. Jones, died only a few weeks before, …

E. C. Faulkner

Searcy, Ark
Arkansas Baptist, April 22, 1896

Rhodes

Rhodes – Frances, only child of Bro. C. B. Rhodes and wife, died on Sunday evening, March 29, after a two weeks' sickness.
She was the only one left of their six children …

A. Hayes.
M. Singer

Clarksville, Ark.
Arkansas Baptist, April 22,1896. page 6

Rhodes

Rhodes Mrs. S. J. Hazen, mother of Frances, wife of Rev. C. B. Rhodes, and our love-adopted mother departed from this world to join her beloved children in eternal peace, April 2, 1896. …

A. Hayes.
M. Singer

Clarksville, Ark.
Arkansas Baptist, April 22, 1896

First part missing

Davidson-Taylor

__ens County, Ala., October 22, 1850; died March 23, 1896, aged 45 years, five months and one day.

Her maiden name was Davidson. … Was married to Elder L. F. Taylor December 31, 1874. Five children blessed this union, three of them preceded by her …

H.A.R.

Arkansas Baptist, April 22, 1896??

Porter

Porter – William H., was born in Coosa County, Georgia, Dec. 14, 1840; died at Trenton, Ark. March 4, 1896, after a long and painful sickness. He came to Phillips County when he was only 9 years old and lived here until the day of his death. He enlisted in the Confederate army in 1861 and served through the war.

On the 22nd of October, 1867, he married Miss Mittie Glass …?

Arkansas Baptist, April 22, 1896

Ryland

Ryland, Mrs. E. Jeanie died in Pine Bluff, Ark., March 26, 1896, aged 32 years. …
To the grief-stricken husband and family…

Mrs. Willis Brown,
Mrs. John Mars,
Mrs. W. D. Brady

Arkansas Baptist, April 22, 1896

Ledbetter

Ledbetter – Florence. With aching heart I record the death of this dear little girl, aged 1 year, 6 months and 20 days. She was drowned in a tub of water that stood under the eave of the house. She was found by her mother, …
her aunt.

Jane Cathey

Chickasawba, Ark.
Arkansas Baptist, May 15, 1896

Rippey

Rippey – Eld. A. J. Born in North Carolina in 1816; moved to South Carolina in 1838; married to Sallie Wofford in 1839; moved to Georgia in 1840; … came to Arkansas in 1870. Died, at the residence of his daughter, Mrs. Black, of Fort Smith, November 6, 1896, aged 80? years. … He leaves two sons and one daughter…

J. W. Nobles,
J. K. Oldham,
J. T. Thomas,
Committee.

Arkansas Baptist, Jan. 6, 1897

Jordan

Jordan, Nannie. Daughter of E. J. Jordan, died at her home in Fordyce, Ark., December 21, 1896. Her death was sudden …

R. D. Wilson.

Fordyce, Ark
Arkansas Baptist, Jan. 6, 1897

Dry

Dry – Jennie F. Born November 13, 18671; married to Jacob M. Dry, September 13, 1888; … Died December 23, 1896, in Jackson County, Ark., and buried in Pleasant Grove cemetery, December 24. The funeral service was conducted by Eld. S. W. Abernethy.

G. B. Borah

Smithville, Ark.
Arkansas Baptist, Jan. 13, 1897

Cantrell

Cantrell – Harriett. Died December 11, 1896. Aged 66 years.
Born in Meigs County, Tenn., in 1830. In her infancy, her parents moved to Hamilton County, and in 1859 she moved to Southern Arkansas and married. Moved to Fulton County in 1891 and resided with her son in law, B. H. Webb, …

James C. Bryan

Arkansas Baptist, Jan. 13, 1897

Atkinson

Atkinson – H. H. Born in Noxubee County, Miss. Sept. 26, 1854. Died at Star City, Ark., Dec. 11, 1896. Aged 42 years, 2 months and 15 days.

Bro. Atkinson came with his parents to Arkansas when but a child. … He leaves a loving wife, three children, two brothers and two sisters …

D. E. Gambrell.

Arkansas Baptist, Jan. 13, 1897

Means

Means – Mrs. Elizabeth. Died at the home of her daughter, Mrs. Thompson, December 6, 1896, aged 79 years, 9 months and 4 days. Born in Greenville District, South Carolina, March 2, 1817; daughter of Henry and Nannie Bradford; moved with her parents to St. Clair County, Ala. , in infancy; married to Andrew N Means, November 23, 1838;… moved with her husband to Calhoun County, Ark., 1853. …

L. D. Miers

Alabama Baptist please copy.
Arkansas Baptist, Jan. 13, 1897

Sayle

Sayle – Dr. W. A. C. Born September, 1835, in Robertson County, Tenn.;… came to Lewisburg (the parent of Morrilton) in [1859]…succumbed to the relentless grasp of consumption, ..
Dec. 30, 1896, leaving his consort and a son, Mr. Claude Sayle, of Little Rock, ..

Giles C. Taylor.

Morrilton.
Arkansas Baptist, Jan. 13, 1897

Cone

Cone - J. B. Born Oct. 12, 1808. Died Oct. 30, 1896, Aged 87 years, 8 days…. born in Washington County, Ga. Moved to Alabama with his parents when very young; he united in marriage to Miss Malinda Dean in Alabama; he professed religion at the age of thirty, at a camp-meeting in Conench County, Alabama;…
 He moved to Arkansas in the year 1852 and reared a large family. …

W. H. Rogers,
D.V. Roney,
R. B. Scott,
Committee

Arkansas Baptist, Jan. 13, 1897

Coffman

Coffman – Laura. Aged 8? Months. Died Jan. 5th, 1897. Buried Jan. 6th, at Portia, Ark., the writer officiating….

Jesse N. Teats.

Black Rock, Ark.
Arkansas Baptist, Jan. 20, 1897

Baldridge

Baldridge – Mrs. Mary C., wife of W. T. Baldridge. Died at Bryant, Arkansas, Dec. 25, 1896; aged 62 years and 8 months.

She was born in Mississippi; reared and married in Tennessee. Moved to Arkansas in 1859 and settled in Saline County. She was the mother of eleven children, eight of whom are left …

Wm. T.

Arkansas Baptist, Jan. 20, 1897

Edie

Edie – Mrs. Levinia (nee Parlmer). Born in Fayette County, Penn., October 5, 1814; died at her home in Judsonia Ark., January 5, 1897; aged 82 years and 3 months_???

On February 2, 1834, she was married to Mr. Thos. Edie, in Ohio, who preceded her in death fourteen years. …\ In 1878 she, with her husband, came to Judsonia, Ark., where she has remained until _____?????

Arkansas Baptist, Jan. 20, 1897

Hoffman

Hoffman – Mrs. Nettie. Died at her home near Arkansas Post, Ark., on December 27, 1896, of consumption….

Arkansas Baptist, Jan. 27, 1897

Hightower

Hightower – David. Born Dec. 1,1884. Died Aug. ;30, 1896; aged 11 years, 8 months and 9 days….

He died at his home at Arkana, Louisiana. …

Arkansas Baptist, Feb. 3, 1897

Berry

Berry – Arthur Wayne. Born in Little Rock, July 32, 1883; died at home, January 13, 1897….

His father J. M. Berry

Central Baptist please copy.

(Affectionately inscribed to the memory of our departed boy, Arthur Wayne, by his father, J.M. Berry.) …

Arkansas Baptist, Feb. 10, 1897

Barnes

Barnes – Dr. R. M. Died February 1, 1897, after an illness of one year.
He was 76 years old…. He leaves a wife, who was very much devoted to him, and one daughter, Mrs. Alice B. Wallis,…

L. Quinn

Charleston, Ark.
Arkansas Baptist, Feb. 17, 1897

Moses

Moses – Dr. E. H., of New Edinburg. Died February 5, 1897. …

B.F. Milam

Arkansas Baptist, Feb. 17, 1897

Willard

Willard – Mrs. E. A. (nee Weaver) _____??? Married at Texarkana, Ark., April, 1888???, at the residence of W. S. C. Gardner, to Jacob Willard, …

J. W. Hubbard

Brownstown, Ark.
Arkansas Baptist, Feb. 17, 1897

Purl

Purl – J. C., died near Bentonville, Ark., January 4,1897, of heart disease. Born in Kentucky December 19, 1824. Lived in Missouri and Kansas many years. About a year ago came to Arkansas. He married Susan Hanks Feb. 22, 1849. She still survives him. Six children were born to them, four of whom survive; Mrs. J. L. Gooding, of Bentonville, Ark.; Mrs. G. W. Lester, of Cripple Creek, Col.; Dr. H. B. Purl of Kirksville, Mo., and Mrs. G. W. Cassidy, of Rochester, N.Y., …

J. T. Moore, Pastor

Arkansas Baptist, Feb. 24,1897

East

East – Mrs. Margaret E., wife of Eld. M. D. East, was born February 11, 1844; died February 9, 1897. Aged 52 years, 11 months and 28 days…. She leaves a husband, two sons and three daughters …

R. P. Bellamy

Imboden, Ark.
Arkansas Baptist, Feb. 24, 1897

Anderson

– Gladys. The subject of this noticed was the daughter of Mr. And Mrs. J. S. Anderson of Arkadelphia. She was born July 20, 1882.

...   EBEM

Arkansas Baptist, March 3, 1897

Kirkland

Kirkland, Catherine. Born in 1845; died December 11, 1896, aged 51. Sister Kirkland was a native of Mississippi; married Eld. W. R. Wood, who died Aug. 6, 1887. On Dec. 13, of the same year, she married Eld. W. J. Kirkland, with whom she lived until Dec. 13, 1896, when she was struck by a passing railroad train and killed….

One of the Bereaved.

Beebe, Ark.

Arkansas Baptist, March 10, 1897

Beck

Beck - C.H. Born Aug. 11, 1825; died Feb. 22, 1897; aged 71 years, 6 months and 11 days….

I. F. Clark

Herndon, Ark.

Arkansas Baptist, March 10, 1897

McIver

– Mathew McIver, son of Archibald and N. A. McIver, was born in Moore County, N. C., December 3, 1847; moved with his parents to Hempstead County, Ark., December, 1851. He was married to Miss S. J. Conway January 9, 1878; … departed this life November 15, 1896.

His sorrowing sister.

Arkansas Baptist, March 10, 1897

Reynolds

Reynolds, Mrs. Mary. Died November 23, 1896, aged 72 years… was born in Tennessee and married to John Reynolds, moved to Texas, from there to Benton County, Ark., ... She was the mother of ten children; five gone before and five remain …

J. S. Spires, Mod. Pro tem
C. C. Mackey, C. C.

Springtown, Ark.

Arkansas Baptist, March 17, 1897

Goodwin

Goodwin, Eld. G. C. Born in Fayette County, Miss., July 11, 1848. Died February 10, 1897. He leaves a wife and four children. He married Sister Susan Pate, November 16, 1869,...

Arkansas Baptist, March 24, 1897

Davis

Davis, Ruth Jane. Wife of Mr. Jas. A. Davis, did at her home in Harrison, January 27, 1897, in the 68th year of her life. ...Besides a host of friends and relatives she leaves a husband and two grown sons.

Rev. Isaac Davis,
J. H. Adair,
Walter H. Dodd,
Committee.

Arkansas Baptist, March 31, 1897

Phillips

Phillips, Sarah Elvira, wife of Mr. Allen Phillips, died at her home near Harrison, of consumption, December 30, 1896. She was born June 4, 1854, Boone County, Arkansas; ...

Rev. Isaac Davis,
J. H. Adair,
Walter H. Dodd,
Committee

Arkansas Baptist, March 31, 1897

Biggadike

Biggadike - Mrs. E. J. Died December 30, 1896, aged 54 years.... born in Ohio, Feb. 10, 1842; married to R. C. Biggadike, Oct. 26, 1868; moved from there to Clark County, Ark., ...

J. T. Howell

Arkansas Baptist, April 7, 1897

Bryant

Bryant, W. A. Died at Fordyce, Ark., March 30, 1897, after a long and severe illness.
Bro. Bryant ... was 75 years old. He lived to see his six children, now living, all grown; and three preceded him ... Of the six who are alive, four are professors.... He was among the first settlers of Dallas County. ...

R. D. Wilson

Arkansas Baptist, April 14, 1897

Kitchens

Kitchens, B. F., on March 5, 1897, at his home, near Gurdon, Ark. Aged. 55 years....He was a native of Arkansas, being born in Clark County, August 10,1841. ...

F. D. Baars

Arkansas Baptist, April 4, 1897

Witham

Witham, W. H. Born in Illinois in Aug., 1844; died in Little River County, Ark., Feb. 23, 1897; aged 52 years.... He married Sister Mary A. Carr in 1865 and moved to Indian Territory in 1894, and returned to Little River County in 1896 ... He leaves a wife, four children and many relatives ...

J. W. Hubbard, Pastor

Arkansas Baptist, April 4, 1897

Cook

Cook, Leon. Died at Buckner, Ark., April 6, 1897, in his 20th year. ...

W. B. Hinton

Arkansas Baptist, April 28, 1897

Wright

Wright, Emma, daughter of C. W. and Della Wright. Born November 6, 1886; died at Alleene, Ark., April 17, 1897. .She leaves a devoted and Christian father and mother, a little brother and many relatives ...

Mattie Daniels

Arkansas Baptist, April 28, 1897

Rice

Rice, B. F. Son of B. F. and Martha Rice, was born in Henry County, Ala., January 14, 1853. Died February 117, 1897, age 44 years, 1 month and 3 days. Moved to Ashley County, Ark., with his parents in 1858; ... He was devoted to mother, brothers and sisters. He leaves a mother, three brothers and four sisters ...That a copy of these resolutions be spread on the minutes of this church, and one be given the *Ashley County Eagle* for publication and one to the Arkansas Baptist,.

J. W. Sims, Moderator,
A. C. Woods, Clerk Pro Tem,
J. M. Gardner,
S. P. Noble

Arkansas Baptist, May 5, 1897

Gist

Gist-J. D. Born July 23, 1849, died March 12, 1897. … He leaves a wife, several small children and a host of friends …

M. T. Webb

Arkansas Baptist, May 12, 1897

Burton

Burton-Chas. A., was born in Henderson County, Tenn., December 19, 1825; …; was married to Nancy H. White January 22, 1852. Sister Burton and five children survive to mourn their loss. … at the ripe age of 71 years, 3 months and 14 days.

M. T. Webb

Arkansas Baptist, May 12, 1897

Richman

Richman-Frances C. Born in Macon County, Tenn., June 1, 1829, died April 20, 1897. She was married to John M. Richman in 1854; … She leaves a husband, six children and a host of friends …

Her pastor,
Eld. W. H. Bowling

Arkansas Baptist, May 12, 1897

Custer

Custerr-Henry Lee. Son of W. P. and Maud Custer, was born in Fulton County, Ark., April 16, 1896. Died May 3, 1897, age 1 year and 17 days. …

W. P. Custer

Arkansas Baptist, June 2, 1897

Broach

Broach-Susan. Was born December 28, 1834. Died September 1, 1896…..

T. W. Branscome,
Sullana Oliver,
N. C. Fry
Committee

Arkansas Baptist, June 2, 1897

Rhodes

Rhodes-Glenn. Aged 2 years, 5 months, and 16 days. … Dr. R. R. Rhodes and wife had watched over their child for near eight months …

R. D. Wilson

Arkansas Baptist, June 2, 1897

King
King-William Carey, in death took the final step in the scale of his ascension to God without a struggle Marcy 21, 1897. He was born in Phillips County, Ark., Aug. 3, 1875. …

F. A. Jeffett

Arkansas Baptist, June 2, 1897

Pickett
Pickett-James R., son of F. G. and Sallie Pickett. Born in Ballard (now Carlisle) County, Ky., June 7, 1856. Died in Lawrence County, Ark., May 2, 1897. Aged 40 years, 10 months and 25 days. … He leaves a wife, several children and other relatives … .

R. B. Bellamy

Arkansas Baptist, June 16, 1897

Byers
Byers-Rubie, oldest daughter of Bro. Lovell and Mary Byers, was born August 22, 1891 and died March 22, 1897, aged 5 years and 7 months….

R. B. Bellamy

Arkansas Baptist, June 16, 1897

Ferguson
Ferguson-Mrs. Antha. Died May 3, 1897, at Pawnee Agency, Oklahoma, aged 54 years. … cared for by a devoted husband and loving children. She leaves a husband, one son and a daughter …

A Friend

Arkansas Baptist, June 30, 1897

Johnson
Johnson-Sheard, at this home near Pleasant Hill church, Hot Spring County, Ark., May 31, 1897. The subject of this sketch was born in Henderson County, Tenn., in 1836. …

Jno. B. Deer

Arkansas Baptist, June 30, 1897

Story
Story – Mary Grace, daughter of Eld. W. R. Story and wife, died June 18, 1897, being 23 years, 8 months and 26 days old….

T. C. Swofford

Arkansas Baptist, July 14, 1897

Whitton
Whittton – Ethel. Born November 11, 1891l; died June 16, 1897. …

E. L. Rushing

Arkansas Baptist, July 4, 1897

Lecroy Lecroy – Thomas. Died at Corwin, Arkansas, aged 84 years. Born in Habersham County, Georgia; …
Arkansas Baptist, July 14, 1897

Shaw
Shaw – W. B. Died near Bland, Ark., May 5, 1897. … the widow, daughter and relatives.…

J. M. Parker
S. A. Milligan
C. B. HendersonCommittee

Arkansas Baptist, July 14, 1897

Stuart
Stuart – R. P. Born in 1825; died June 25, 1897. Aged 72 years. …He leaves two married daughters and several grandchildren to mourn his death.

T.M. Rowlans
C. McMurray
G. T. Sykes
Committee.

Fordyce, Ark.
Arkansas Baptist, July 14, 1897

Redditt
Redditt – Rebecca. Born November 30, 1846. Died Jun 22, 1897. Aged 50 years, 6 months and 22 days.
Sister Redditt was born in Alabama, came to Arkansas\ in 1857, …

J. W. Outlaw

Oil Trough, Ark.
Arkansas Baptist, July 14, 1897

Gowin
Gowin – Cassie. A daughter of C. A. and L. A. Gowin, died at Hoyt, I.T. Aged 18 years. Gone to join her mother, who died 18 months ago. Cassie as born at Cedarville, Arkansas. …

C. A. Gowin

Hoyt, Ark.
Arkansas Baptist, July 23/28???, 1897

Powell

Powell – At her home near Charleston, Ark. Annie Powell died May 19, 1897. Born in Jackson County, Virginia, July 2, 1868....

Thomas J. Flynn

Charleston, Ark .
Arkansas Baptist, July 23/28?:? 1897

Porter

Porter – Miss Anna Lee. Resolutions of respect. ...
Arkansas Baptist, July 23/28??, 1897

Hunt-Jackson

Jackson-Mrs. S. A., whose maiden name was Hunt, was born September 25, 1825, in Spartanburg, S.C.; moved to Panola County, Miss. In 1838; ... She was married to S. W. Jackson in 1851; moved to Brownsville in 1856, thence to Dardanelle in 1859, where she passed from this life July 12, 1897. Her husband went on before her some twenty-five years ago. ...

A. H. Autry

Arkansas Baptist, Aug. 4, 1897

Moffitt

Moffitt-Matilda, wife of C. V. Moffitt. Born January 24, 1849; died June 20, 1886, at Reyno. ...

E. T. Lincoln

Arkansas Baptist, Aug. 4, 1897

Woodson

Woodson-Walter C., son of W. M. and Mattie Woodson, near Bellville, Ark., July 8, 1897. Aged 1 year, 7 months and 9 days....

Luna Spiller

Danville, Ark.
Arkansas Baptist, Aug. 11, 1897

Dean

Dean-Lucy, daughter of John Sweat, and wife of Wm. Dean. Born in Mississippi, October 10, 1875; came to this State when a child ... Married Wm. Dean January 15, 1897, with whom she lived happy until her death which occurred July 28, 1897, at her home near Weldon, Ark. She leaves a farther, husband, brother, sister and a host of friends ...

E. I. Martin

Arkansas Baptist, August 11, 1897

Slater
Slater-Guy Hatley, died July 27, 1897, at Judsonia, Ark., of typhoid malaria. Aged 14 years and ten days....

Mr. A and Mrs. F. A. Slater

Arkansas Baptist, August 11, 1897

Maxwell
Maxwell-Myra L., daughter of John and Amanda Thornton Maxwell. Born September 20, 1874, in Tate County, Miss.;...

E. C. Faulkner

Baptist Record and Baptist Reflector are requested to copy.
Arkansas Baptist, August 11, 1897

Bradford
Bradford-Nancy. Born Jan. 16, 1874, died July 19, 1897....

M. E. Millikin,
W. R. Underwood,
H. A. Seal,
Committee

Arkansas Baptist, August 18, 1897

Allen
Allen-Francis E., nee Rushing, wife of Eld. Hogan Allen, died at her home near Hamburg Ark., July 28, 1897. ...
Arkansas Baptist, August 18, 1897

Littlefield
Littlefield. Elizabeth. Born October, 1812, died August 5, 1897.... She leaves six children bereaved, ...

R. G. Thomas

Arkansas Baptist, August 25, 1897

Lay
Lay, W. L. Born in Scott County, Tenn. August 1, 1876. He came to this State in March, 1888; ... He leaves a mother, three brothers, three sisters and many friends ...

R. A. Smith

Arkansas Baptist, August 25, 1897

Daniel
Daniel-J. J., died at Fordyce, Ark., Aug. 17, 1897. Aged 42 years, 4 months and 4 days. ...

R. D. Wilson

Arkansas Baptist, Sept. 1, 1897

Daniels
Daniels-Jennie Lee, infant son of H. N. and Ida Daniels, near Brinkley, Ark. Departed this life August 2, 1897. ...

Mama and Papa

Arkansas Baptist, Sept. 1, 1897

Somers
Somers-Mrs. Adeline E., daughter of Rev. J. C. and Mrs. L. J. Russell. Died August 8, near Humphrey, Ark. Aged 19 years....

Mamma

Arkansas Baptist, Sept. 15, 1897

Atkinson
Atkinson-Mrs. A. J., died August 15, 1897, at Star City, Ark., aged 65 years and 3 months.... She leaves two sons, four daughters, three sons-in-law, seventeen grandchildren, two brothers and a host of relatives and friends ...

D. E. Gambrell

Arkansas Baptist, Sept. 15, 1897

Harley
Harley-Milton, Son of Eld. W. C. Harley. Died a Barkada, Ark., June 26, 1897, aged 22 years, 3 months and 12 days. ...

C. W. Barker,
J. R. Wallace,
S. A. Roark,
H. N. King,
Committee

Arkansas Baptist, Sept. 15, 1897

Jones
Jones-Hon. A. C. Born January 1826 in Halifax County, Va. At the age of 9, his parents moved to Carroll County, Tenn. In 1853, he came to Warren, Ark., and in 1856 was married to Mrs. D. C. Wells. ... until his death, which occurred on July 10, 1897. ...

C.C. Gannaway,
W. F. Mack,
M. E. Hughey,
M. T. Gill,
O'Neal,
N. C. Denson,
Committee

Arkansas Baptist, Sept. 15, 1897

Meadows

Meadows-Mrs. Mary. Died Sept. 14, 1897, near Osceola, Ark; aged 75 years and 23 days. Mrs. Meadows was born and reared in South Carolina, and moved to Tennessee in 1870. In 1885 she moved to Mississippi County, Ark., ... She leaves four sons, one daughter, many relatives and a host of friends ..

M. M.

Arkansas Baptist, Sept. 20?, 1897

Cardin

Cardin – Rachael, whose maiden name was Mitchell, was born January 11, 1808, in North Carolina, and moved to Coffey County, Tenn., when a small child. She was married to Robert Cardin in 1829. There were born unto them ten children, two of whom died in infancy; .... Five went before her; five to follow. Her husband preceded her in death 24 years, leaving her alone ... lived to be nearly ninety years old. She fell asleep in Jesus Saturday morning, September 4. ...

Arkansas Baptist, Sept. 20?, 1897

Hill

Hill-Mrs. Mary L. Died at her home in Malvern, Ark., September 24, 1897, at 10 o'clock. The deceased was born in Taylorsville, Ky., October 31, 1830. ... She was married to John S. Hill in early womanhood. They resided in Kentucky, Illinois, Kansas and then came to Arkansas about nine years ago. ... She was stricken with paralysis, and in two days died. She leaves a husband, three sons and one daughter to mourn ...

Mrs. C. R. Adams

Western Recorder please copy.
Arkansas Baptist, Oct. 13, 1897

Young

Young-Eld. John M., was born in Madison County, Tenn., in 1828. After he attained his growth he went to Alabama and remained three years. While there he married Miss Emaline Simms, and later went to Georgia and remained about twenty years. In 1870 he moved to Logan County, Ark. In February, 1880, his wife died, leaving nine children to brighten the life of the bereaved father. About a year later, he married Miss Prude Rana. He died at his home in Revilee valley, January 28, 1897, leaving his wife and thirteen children to mourn his death. ...

Arkansas Baptist, Oct. 20, 1897

Staggs
Staggs-Mrs. Ann; died Oct. 7, 1897, near Donaldson, Ark. Her maiden name was Bell; she was born in Alabama, … She leaves one child and a host of grandchildren and friends …

Jennie Jones

Arkansas Baptist, Oct., 27, 1897
Yeager
Yeager, Eld. J. G. – Born in Miss. Sept. 23, 1823. Died in Texas August 20, 1897.
Bro. Yeager moved to Dallas County, Ark., …

J. L. Hogg
T. C. Heard
R. B. Devine
C. M. Myrick, Com.

New Hope Church, Dallas, Co.
Arkansas Baptist, Oct. 27, 1897

Phillips
Phillips-R.A. Born May 5, 1853, in Louisiana and died October 10? 1897? Moved to Arkansas at the age of 15. Was married to Dora Preston October 12, 1887. … He leaves a wife and four children, relatives and friends to mourn …

W. S. C. Gardner
H. G. Sanderson
J. W. Hubbard
Committee

Arkansas Baptist, October 27, 1897

Winn
Winn-Alice – The following tribute of respect to the memory of Alice Winn, was approved by the Judsonia Baptist Sunday School Sunday morning Oct. the 17th 1897: …In the sudden death of our esteemed Sister Alice Winn on board the English Steamer *Bathurst* anchored at Axim West Africa, …
Arkansas Baptist, Oct. 27, 1897

Spotts
Spotts, Mary –This sister departed this life September 7, 1897, at the advanced age of 70 years, one month and ten days. … She leaves three sons and one daughter and a number of grandchildrenand other relatives and friends …

R. B. Bellamy

Arkansas Baptist, November 3, 1897

Kirtland

Kirtland, George – This brother departed this life October 12, 1897, aged 23 years, seven months and ten days. He was a teacher by profession … He leaves a father and mother and one sister to mourn …

R. B. Bellamy

Arkansas Baptist, Nov. 3, 1897

O'Neall

Thursday, October 14, Mr. J. H. O'Neall was called to lay down the pain and care of this life … He leaves a wife, three daughters, and four sons to mourn his absence from their home.
They brought him and laid him beside his well-beloved daughter, our Miss O'Neall who left us a little more than a year ago. …

Mrs. J. G. Lile
Central College

Arkansas Baptist, Nov. 10, 1897

Richardson

Richardson-Freddie. Son of J. A. and Arrie E. Richardson; born September 12, 1896; died October 20, 1897. …

Lucy Browning,
Gertrude Perry

Heber.
Arkansas Baptist, Nov. 10, 1897

In memory of Sue Bull

Bull

Little Sue, daughter of Mr. and Mrs. John G. Bull, was born in Union County, Ark., on September 3, 1884, moved with her parents to Hot Spring County February 13, 1891, and died October 14, 1897. …

Jno. C. Ross,
Alice Dyer,
Bessie Noble, Com.

Adopted by Malvern Sunday-school, October 24, 1897.

Dollar

Dollar – Rosena P., wife of D. L. Dollar; born in Pulaski County, Tenn., in 1846; died September 17, 1897. …Judsonia?
Arkansas Baptist, Nov._____ 1897

Birmingham

Birmingham-Mrs. Elizabeth was born August 25, 1853; … till God called her September 25, 1897. She leaves a husband and six children…

J. F. C.

Arkansas Baptist, Nov. 24, 1897

McCall

McCall-Eld. J. N., was born October 6, 1842. Departed this life February 18, 1897. …He leaves a wife and six children, and an old mother of 98 years, one brother and sister, …

Rev. J. F. Clark

Herndon
Arkansas Baptist, Nov. 24, 1897

Kenady

Kenady-Mrs. Alice. Born in Lamar County, Texas, Oct. 3, 1876. Daughter of Henry Myers. She was born from above in 1889, … She leaves a broken-hearted husband and two little girls. …

Her devoted sister,
Lou Nelson

Bierne, Ark.
Arkansas Baptist, Dec. 1, 1897

Dillard

Dillard, Dr. Henry Thomas, was born December 20, 1853, in DeSoto Parish, Louisiana. A few years of his early life were spent in Texas. He returned to Louisiana in 1860. After studying medicine in New York he gave his attention to that noble calling….. He moved to North Little Rock from Shreveport in 1895 … for he was taken worse at the residence of Mr. W. C. Armstrong, his brother-in-law, twelve miles from Little Rock, and after twelve weeks of suffering, he passed away Friday night, November 26?. …
Arkansas Baptist, Dec. 18??, 1897

O'Neal
In Memory of J.H. O'Neal
…

Mrs. J. H. Colyear
Mrs. S. B. Barham
Mrs. J. H. Ciferd
Committee

St. Francis
Arkansas Baptist, Dec. 15, 1897

Coleman
Eld. R. J. Coleman ...

A. J. Wharton

Millican, Texas
Arkansas Baptist, Dec. 22, 1897

In Memoriam....

Perminter
J. B. Perminter, on the 14th inst., after a painful illness of three weeks; ... a copy of these resolutions be published in the Forrest City Times and Democrat, and also in the Arkansas Baptist, and Review.

W. H.? P_____
J. M. Prewett
W. T. Sanders

Arkansas Baptist,?, Dec. 22, 1897

DeLaughter
DeLaughter-Mrs. Nannie (Vanderslice). Born in Dallas County, Ark., November 1, 1862; died December 9, 1897. Her life was spent here, except eight years in Nashville, Tenn. ... She was married to Rev. Benjamin DeLaughter June , 1896; ...

A Friend

Arkansas Baptist, Jan. 12, 1898

Poe
Poe – Mrs. Martha? Died at Russellville, Ark., Dec. 3,1 897. Aged 82 years. Sister Poe was born in North Carolina, and moved to Grant County, Arkansas, over forty years ago. For several years after the war she lived in Little Rock, and kept the Poe Hotel on Fifth street. Her daughter married Bro. A. T. Davis, of Russellville, and in recent years she made her home there. ...
Arkansas Baptist, Jan. 12, 1898

Moore
Moore-Miss Lettie. Died in Little Rock, December 30, 1897. Aged 20 yeas and months. ...
Arkansas Baptist, Jan. 19, 1898

Smith
Smith-William Henry. Killed by a falling shed, January 5, 1898. Aged 21 years and 4 months. ...

J. H.Reynolds,
Nettie McKay,
M. May Clark,
Committee

Arkansas Baptist, Jan. 19, 1898

Looney
Looney, W. C. Died at his home near Mt. Comfort, Washington County, Arkansas, January 2, 1898. Aged 55 years, 1 month and 29 days.
Bro. Looney was born at Nashville, Tenn.... In 1882 he moved to Crawford County, Arkansas; thence to Washington County, where he died. ... Bro. Looney had suffered the last five years of his life from a stroke of paralysis. .. He leaves a grief-stricken widow and five children to mourn their loss.

A Friend and Brother

Arkansas Baptist, Jan.19, 1898

Mosley
Mosley-W.A., died at the home of his son, W. T. Moseley, January 9, 1898. Aged 96 years and 7 days. He moved from South Carolina to Arkansas in 1850, and lived on the same place ever since. He had been a member of the Baptist church for 50 years; ...

Sister Youngblood
W. H. Cash

Toledo.?
Arkansas Baptist, Jan. 19, 1898

Watson
Watson-James Oscar. He was the eldest son of John O. and Fannie Watson. He was born October 28, 1874, and died December 30, 1897. at his home near Brownsville, Ark., where most of his halcyon days of childhood and the golden days of boyhood were spent. ...
Arkansas Baptist, Jan. 19, 1898

Rogers
Rogers- B. L. ... December 28, 1897, ...
 was born in Carroll County, Mississippi, November 22, 1831; came from there and located in Ashley County, Arkansas, in 1861; ...

J. W. Sims

Arkansas Baptist, Jan. 26, 1898

Todd/DoddTodd?
Dodd?-Alvis. Mount Olive Baptist church, Guy, Ark., adopted the following resolutions December 4, 1897:

H. P. ? Glover,
J. P. Kessinger,
Committee

Arkansas Baptist, Jan. 20, 1898

Lester
Lester – J. J. Resolutions on the death of Hon. J. J. Lester, of Atkins, Ark., who died at his home December 2, 1897. … That we tender sympathy and help to the bereaved and stricken wife and children and relatives …
Arkansas Baptist, Jan. 26, 1898.

Freeman
Freeman- F., died on March 12, 1895. Aged 69 years, 9 months and 9 days. Bro. Freeman was born in Ray County, Tenn., June 8, 1825. …He was married to Elizabeth Sidley, who preceded him about four years. … He leaves a host of friends and relatives to mourn
their loss – God bless his children ..

W. N. Womack

Morrison's Bluff, Ark.
March 4, 1895

Adcock
Adcock – J. D., died on March 4, 1895. …

C. M. Powell

March 4, 1895

Barnett
Barnett, Ellen E., died at her home in Van Buren County, Ark., March 25, 1895, aged 12 years, 2 months and 25 days.
Ellen was born in Etowah County, Alabama, Dec. 29, 1882. She was moved several times, and was finally brought to Van Buren County, Ark., in December, 1890. … She leaves a father and mother, four brothers, one sister, and a host of friends … B. Barnett

Her Brother

March 4, 1895

Johnson

Death has again taken from our membership our beloved brother, Eld. W. C. Johnson, who departed this life on Thursday, January 17, 1895?. … He was 72 years old….

S. H. Weatherly,
John Hammett,
W. T. Allison, committee
Holliday, Ark.

March 4, 1895

Lett

Lett, Mrs. T. B. died at her home in Little Rock on February 6, 1895. …

Frank White

March 13, 1895

Gunter

Gunter – Eld. James, died at his home on Copeland Ridge January 6, 1896. – Aged 71 years. …

J. A. Hardage,
D. A. Johnston,
B. W. Wright, Committee

March 13, 1895

Harris

Harris – Augustine, died in Cleburne, Texas, March 12, 1895. Aged 71 years and 8 months…. He was born in North Carolina in 1823; moved to Georgia … later he moved to Northern Arkansas, where he stayed for several years. Two years ago he came to Texas to live with his son, Dr. T. T. Harris, at whose home he died. His son, Eld. Wm. H. Harris, and a younger son in attendance upon a medical school in St. Louis, came to join their two brothers here in administering to …

J. W. Newbrough

Cleburne, Tex.
April 10, 1895

Alford

Alford - Lucy, died at her home in Sparkman, Ark., March 27, 1895. … May the husband and three grown children find comfort ….

H. J. P. Horne

April 10, 1895

Quinn

Quinn – Mrs. Nettie, wife of T. W. Quinn, died at her home near Prattsville, Ark., January 30, 1895. Aged 40 years….. She called her husband and two children to her deathbed and, …

A Friend…

April 10, 1895

Lindsey

Lindsey – R. E. Lee, son of Eld. R.? H. Lindsey, died of consumption March 29, 1895….
Paper missing
April 10, 1895

Bonner

Bonner – Anna, daughter of J. A. and Dalia Bonner, died April 7, 1895. Aged 17 years, 8 months and 25 days.
Sister Anna was born in Randolph County, Ala., December 13, 1877. …

Her Pastor

April 16, 1895

MARRIAGES

Little-Terry
At the residence of the bride's father, on the 8th Dec. 1859, by his excellency, Elias N. Conway, Governor of the State of Arkansas, Mr. Robert A. Little to Miss Sallie A. Terry, daughter of Dr. W. S. Terry, all of Pulaski County.
Arkansas Baptist, Dec. 16, 1859

Jones-Pearce
Married, on the 25th of July 1860 in Ouachita County, Ark., by Elder G. W. Scroggin, Mr. Elisha L. M. Jones (son of James Jones), and Miss Fredonia A. Pearce, (daughter of L. D. Pearce), all of the above County.
Arkansas Baptist, Aug. 8, 1860

McEloy-Hall
Married – at Mineral Springs, Arkansas, on the 13th of May, by Rev. Jno. C. Shipp, Miss Eura McEloy? to Mr. A. Britt Hall, formerly of Michigan.
Western Baptist, May 29, 1875?

Rodgers-Bevens
Married on the 2d instant, by Elder N. H. Owen, Mr. W. T. Rodgers and Miss Katie Bevens, all of White County, Arkansas.
Western Baptist, May 29, 1875?

Monroe-Gallion
On Sunday, January 1, 1876, at the residence of Samuel Story, by Eld. Thos. Poostelle, Eld. Edward Monroe and Miss Annie Gallion.
Western Baptist, Jan. 20, 1876

Daman-Shilling
At the residence of the brides father, on the 2nd inst. By Eld. M. Green, J. W. Daman and Miss A. J. Shilling, all of White County, Ark.
Mr. Daman found a Shilling near Judsonia. He claimed it, and on the 2nd of January, I gave him a legal right to hold it forever.
G.
Western Baptist, Jan. 20, 1876

Ellis-Hamilton

At the residence of Mr. Boyle by Esquire W. S . Knox, Mr. Wm. M. Ellis and Miss Mary E. Hamilton, all of White County.

Western Baptist, Jan. 27, 1876

Hogue-Barnes

On the 5th day of January, at the residence of the bride's father, by Eld. F. F. D. Sheffy, Mr. A. Y. Hogue and Miss T. A. Barnes, all of White County.

Western Baptist, Jan. 27, 1876

Fowlkes-Arnold

On the 13th of January, at the residence of the bride's father, by Eld. J.F. D. Shefy,. Mr. H. E. H. Fowlkes and Miss Lucinda E. Arnold, all of White County, Ark.

Western Baptist, Jan. 27, 1876

Davis-Anderson

At the residence of the bride, on the 8th inst., by Eld. T. P. Boone, Mr. W. H. Davis and Mrs. Ellen Anderson, all of Little Rock, Ark.

Western Baptist, March 12, 1876

Atkins-Wheless

At he residence of the bride's father, by Rev. N. C. Denson, at 9 A.M. January 6th, 1884, Mr. Wm. N. Atkins of Dorsey County, to Miss Mollie Wheless, of Warren, Arkansas.

After congratulation, Mr. Atkins and his bride left for their future home in Annover, Dorsey County, carrying with them the best wishes of many friends.

A. Friend.

A.B.? Apr. 17, 1884

Ives-Glaze

In Little Rock, February 28, 1886, by S. Cornelius, D. D., Mr. J. H. Ives, and Miss Annie Glaze, both of Owen township, Pulaski County.

Arkansas Baptist, March 11, 1886

Bodeman-Benedict

In Little Rock, March, 1886, by S. Cornelius, D. D., Mr. B. Bodeman, and Mrs. M .E. Benedict, all of Little Rock.

Arkansas Baptist, March 11, 1886

Danberry-Swain
In Little Rock February 18, 18786. By S. Cornelius, D. D., Mr. G. F. Danberry and Mrs. Nervaney Swain, all of Little Rock.
Arkansas Baptist, March 11, 1886

Miles-Watson
Rev. O. P. Miles, of Grand Lake and Miss Cora Watson, of Hamburgh, Ark., were married on the 12th of August. The ceremonies were performed by Rev. J. B. Wise, of Bastrop, La.
Arkansas Baptist, Sept. 3, 1885

Brown-Nuckler
Elder J. L. Brown was married to Miss Mary E. Nuckler at the bride's father on the evening of March 2d, 1886, Elder J. J. Martin officiating.
Subscribe for the Arkansas Evangel.
Arkansas Baptist, April 1, 1886

Hughes-Deacon
L. B. Hughes, near Johnson, Arkansas, **March 25, 1890.**

Thomas-Martin
At the home of the bride's mother, 402 W. Fourth avenue, Pine Bluff, Ark., Miss Bertie Martin and Mr. Clement Thomas, C. F. J. Tate, the bride's Pastor, officiating.
Arkansas Baptist, Jan. 6, 1897

McIlwain-Shapard
At the Gleason Hotel, Little Rock, Ark., Dec. 23, 1896, J. W. McIlwain, principal of the Morrilton Graded Schools, and Miss Vestal Shapard, also of Morrilton, the editor of the Arkansas Baptist officiating. May they lie to celebrate their golden wedding, is our prayer.
Arkansas Baptist, Jan. 6, 1897

Lyle-Jacks
At the residence of Mrs. Sarah E. Jacks, Helena, Ark., Jan. 6, 1897, Mr. James B. Lyle, and Miss Bettie Jacks. Sorry we could not accept invitation to be present, but we do wish them a happy, prosperous life-journey together.
Arkansas Baptist, Jan. 6, 1897

Puddephatt-Murdough

Charles H. Puddephatt and Miss Bessie Murdough, at Pine Bluff, February 3, 1897, by Pastor C. E. J. Tate, Bro. Puddephatt is one of our prosperous young business men, who makes his business honor the Lord, and the bride is an attractive young lady of superior attainments endowed with qualities to make her a worthy helpmate? May their lives be bright and God be glorified in them.

Arkansas Baptist, Feb. 17, 1897

Culpepper-Evans

At the Second Baptist church, Little Rock, Sunday, February 14, at 3:30 p.m. Mr. J. W. Culpepper of Pine Bluff, and Miss Ella Evans of Little Rock, Eld. J. W. Fletcher officiating. After the marriage they went at once to their future home in Pine Bluff.

Arkansas Baptist, Feb. 17, 1897

Olcott-Clegg

At the home of the bride's parents, 1121 West Barraque Street, Pine Bluff, Ark., at 4:15 p.m. Sunday, April 11, 1897, Mr. H. T. Olcott and Miss Lizzie Clegg, by Pastor C. F. J. Tate. Mr. and Mrs. Olcott left immediately for a three weeks' visit among relatives in Indiana. They are of the best young people of our city and will receive a royal welcome upon their return.

Arkansas Baptist, April 14, 1897

Kidd-Files

At the Second church in Little Rock, Tuesday at 4 p.m., April 29, Miss Ethel Ray Files, daughter of Hon. A. W. Files, president of the Arkansas Baptist State Board, and R. A. Kidd of Wilmar, Ark. May a long, happy life be theirs.

April 29, 1897

Cannon-Lile

At the residence of J. R. Lile, Lumber, Ark., June 7, 1897, Mr. G. E. Cannon, of Hempstead County, Ark., and Miss Josie Lile, of this place, Eld. L. O Oxford officiating. The ceremony was beautiful and impressive. Miss Lile is a sister of Prof J. G. Lile, president of Central Baptist college, Conway, Ark. She is a graduate of Central college with B.S. honors. Mr. Cannon is one of the leading young Christian men of Arkansas and a graduate of Ouachita college and of Louisville Medical college. We wish them a happy, successful future, with abundant blessing from God's bountiful hand.

Arkansas Baptist, June 16, 1897

Galloway-Cleveland
At the home of the bride's brother, Pine Bluff, Ark., at high noon June 8, 1897, Mr. D. M. Galloway and Miss Annie Cleveland, Pastor C. F. J. Tate, officiating. The bride has for years been leading soprano of the First Baptist choir and will be greatly missed from religious and social circles. The groom is a prominent businessman of Nashville, Ark., where the couple will make

 their home, after spending a fortnight at the Tennessee Centennial.
Arkansas Baptist, June 16, 1897

Cole-Phillips
At Mossy Creek, Tenn., August 16, 1897, Mr. W. D. Cole, of Conway, Ark., and Miss Laura A. Phillips, daughter of Rev. J. M. and Mrs. Lucy Dayton Phillips. Mr. Cole is a prosperous merchant in Conway and Miss Phillips has been a popular teacher in Central College for two years. They have the well wishes of the *Arkansas Baptist,*. May a long length of life and great prosperity be theirs.
Arkansas Baptist, June 23, 1897

Morgan-Lloyd
In   Pine   Bluff
, 2 p.m., Sunday, June 20, 1897????, by ____F.J. Tate, Mr. John Morgan ???? Pastor C. __ Lloyd. Contracting parties and Mrs. May _____ are well and favorably known.
Arkansas Baptist, June 23, 1897

Jones-Cannon
At the Trulock Hotel, Pine Bluff, Ark., Sunday, Nov. 21, at 3 p.m., Prof. W.M. Jones, principal of the Star City schools, and Miss Mollie Cannon, teacher in Mena public school, N. C. Denson officiating. He is a graduate of Ouachita, and she of Central College.
The bride is the daughter of Eld. B. F. Cannon of Silver City, Arkansas. May no clouds darken the bright prospects before them.
Arkansas Baptist, Nov. 24, 1897

McDonald-Owens

Never did a convention close more uniquely. As the president was speaking his farewell words, pending the vote to adjourn, Eld. J. W. McDonald, of Hot Springs, and Miss Grace Truman Owens, of Monticello, stepped on the platform and Dr. S. H. Ford, in his inimitable manner, performed the religious and Bro. Eagle the legal ceremony, making them husband and wife. They then joined in the closing hand-shaking and what was to the convention the parting hand, was to give the hand clasp of "God be with you" to the end. To which the ARKANSAS BAPTIST, says, Amen.

Arkansas Baptist, Nov. 24, 1897

Black-Patton

Married at the residence of the bride's father, W. M. Patton, in Cabot, Lonoke County, Ark., on April 24, 1894, Mr. J. F. Black of Little Rock, with the firm of Bradshaw & Cunningham, and Miss Jo Patton. Ceremonies performed y Eld. R. J. Coleman.

   May the Lord bless the union and make them useful in His vineyard.

R.J.C.

Arkansas Baptist, May 8,1895

Ticer-Roger[s]

On the evening of March 28, at the residence of Mr. Henry Cotton, of Turner, Ark., Mr. J. C. Ticer and Miss Lula Rogers were united in the holy bonds of matrimony, J. J. Day, officiating. May their lives be one of peace and happiness.

M. J. Day

Arkansas Baptist, March 5, 1895,

Little-Holland

At the residence of the bride's sister, March 5, at 3 p.m., Mr. Daniel Little and Miss Thulia Holland. The writer officiating. The bride is an efficient member of Union Baptist church.

W. F. Bridges

March 25, 1896

Munn-Gannaway

At the residence of the bride's father, Dr. C. C. Gannaway, in Warren, Ark., at 8:30 a.m., March 17, 1896, Eld. Hector A. Munn and Miss Mary Nina Gannaway. Eld. N. C. Denson officiating. Bro. Munn is pastor of Warren and Kingsland churches, and Miss Nina is one of the most estimable young ladies in Southeast Arkansas. Bro. Munn is a staunch friend of THE BAPTIST, and the editor congratulates him on his success. May a long life of bliss attend their career.

March 25, 1896

Holmes-Hollis

At the residence of Judge Hollis, Mr. Pitt Holmes, of Kingsland, Ark., and Miss Birdie Hollis, Orlando, Ark., Dec. 12, 1895. H. A. Munn officiating. We wish these young people a pleasant voyage through life.

H. A. M.

Index